D1091355

Ancient Britons

Ancient Britons

How They Lived

pictures by

MARJORIE MAITLAND HOWARD

text by

HENRY HODGES and

EDWARD PYDDOKE

PRAEGER PUBLISHERS

New York · Washington

BOOKS THAT MATTER

Published in the United States of America in 1970
by Praeger Publishers, Inc.
111 Fourth Avenue, New York, N.Y. 10003

Library of Congress Catalog Card Number: 79-96770

Printed in Great Britain

CONTENTS / TIME SCALE

MAN THE HUNTER

The Earliest Stone Age or Lower Palaeolithic Period
(250,000 to 80,000 years ago)

The Later Old Stone Age or Upper Palaeolithic Period
(80,000 to 10,000 years ago)

The Middle Stone Age or Mesolithic Period
(10,000 BC to 3,000 BC)

MAN THE FARMER

The New Stone Age or Neolithic Period
(3,000 BC to 1,600 BC)

CONTENTS / TIME SCALE *continued*

THE COMING OF METALS

The Copper Age (1,600 BC *to 1,400* BC*)*

The Bronze Age (1,400 BC *to 500* BC*)*

The Iron Age (500 BC *to* AD *43)*

THE ROMANS

(Julius Caesar 55 BC *to Claudius Caesar Augustus* AD *43)*

Ancient Britons

This book tries to describe simply what has been found out about the ordinary life of men, women and children who lived in our part of the world before writing was known. Marjorie Maitland Howard in her drawings has added flesh and blood to our words.

It is now possible for many details of life in prehistoric times to be filled in; archaeologists must always stick to facts, but research, deduction and experiment are making more and more of the parts of the jig-saw fit into place.

So far as possible we have tried to leave out technical terms and dates, but for the benefit of those who would like to fit the chapters of our book into the usual range of periods and dates we have added a short table (the Time Scale in the Contents List on the previous two pages).

Immense periods of time are involved and, between the time when the earliest known men hunted in the forests and the time when the Romans first came to Britain's shores, 250 million years passed.

The climate changed several times: the greater part of Britain was covered twice with glaciers and sheet-ice, the sea has changed its level and rivers have cut down their channels and even changed their courses; but, on the changing landscape, the men and women whose lives we have described have left clues and traces.

It can be exciting to find these relics of a distant past and then to recognise and understand burial mounds, hill-forts and even indications of the former existence of fields, villages and towns. They are all common features in many parts of our countryside, for the past is not easily rubbed out.

E. P.
H. H.

Man the Hunter

PEOPLE OF THE OLD STONE AGE

A quarter of a million years ago the coastline of Britain was very different from today. There was no English Channel and Britain was still part of the Continent. For a long warm period between two phases of the Ice Age the waters of the sea were at a higher level than they are now and the rivers had not yet cut down to their present beds. In these remains of the higher sands and shingles, of the beaches of these ancient seas, and the gravels of the early river-beds, we find clues to the former existence of men of the Old Stone Age.

These traces consist largely of stone tools, for nothing lasts so long as stone, though these ancestors of ours were clever enough to have made other implements of wood and bone.

These stone tools were made by breaking and chipping rough lumps of flint and other rock until what was left had a useful shape. Some of them, for convenience, have been called 'hand-axes', but they must have been used for a number of different purposes – skinning animals, digging for edible roots and for all kinds of work for which things had to be cut or shaped. The men of the Old Stone Age were able to make, besides 'hand-axes', all manner of scraping tools and sharp wedges, which we call 'cleavers'.

Along with these implements of stone we find also in the sands and gravels the bones of animals, some of which were hunted and trapped for their skins and for eating. Since the climate was warm we find the bones of animals such as a large straight-tusked elephant, a two-horned rhinoceros, bison and large cattle. All these roamed freely over the Continent of Europe into what is now Britain.

So far as we can guess these early men were not great inventors and they continued to live as their ancestors for tens of thousands of years, hunting and collecting nuts, roots and berries, very much as Australian aborigines do to this day.

Our main picture shows an early man, such as the one whose skull was found at Swanscombe in Kent, chipping a block of flint to make a hand-axe. In the background can be seen the great straight-tusked elephant.

Swanscombe, Kent. Chipping a flint to make a hand-axe.

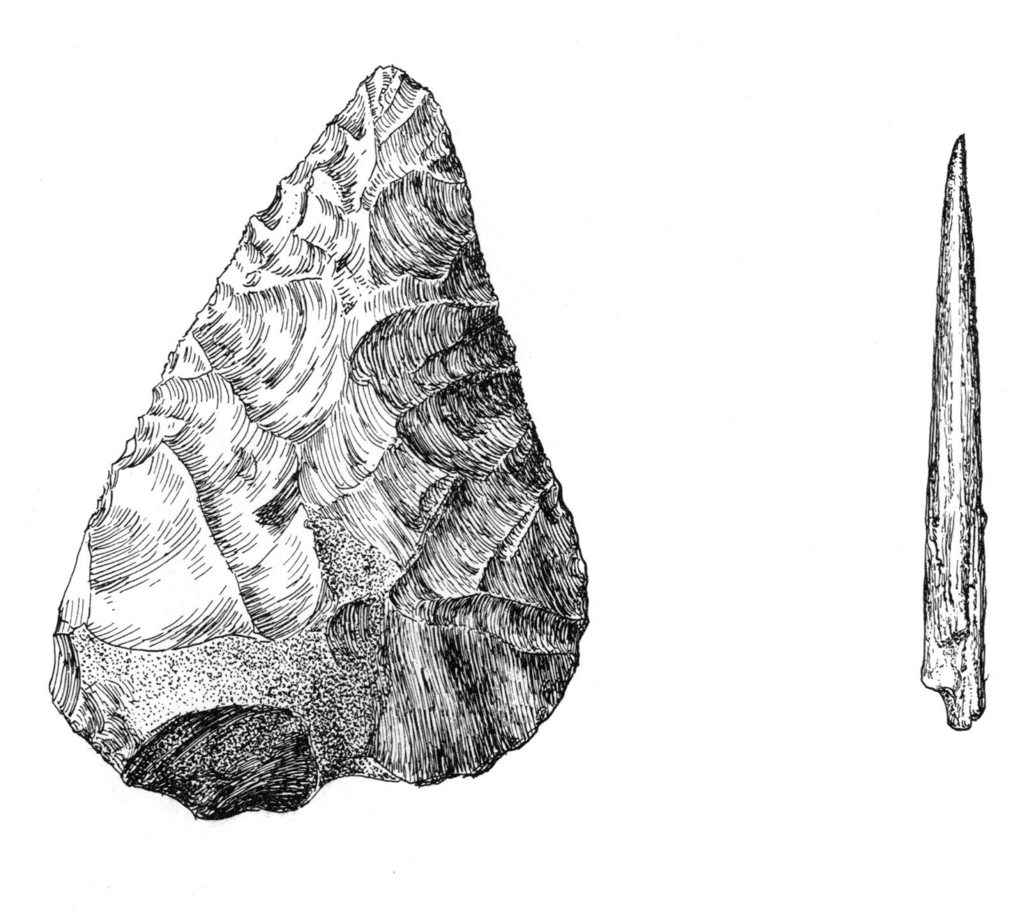

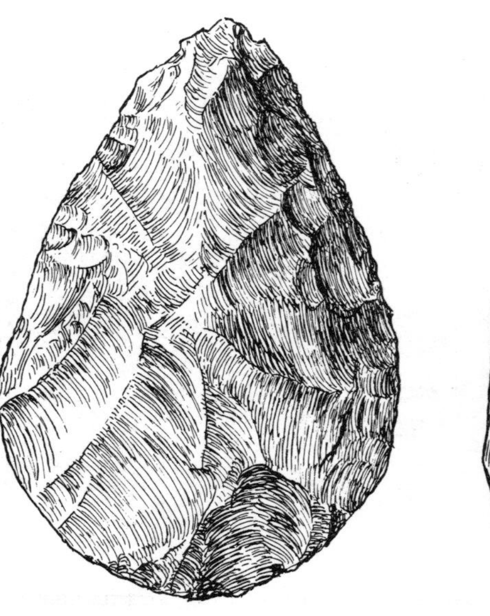

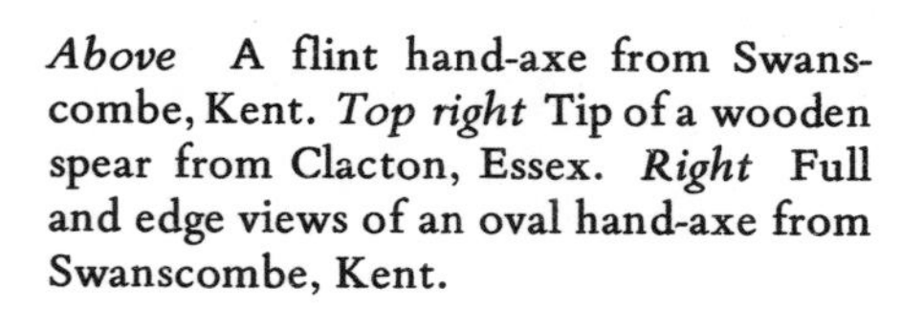

Above A flint hand-axe from Swanscombe, Kent. *Top right* Tip of a wooden spear from Clacton, Essex. *Right* Full and edge views of an oval hand-axe from Swanscombe, Kent.

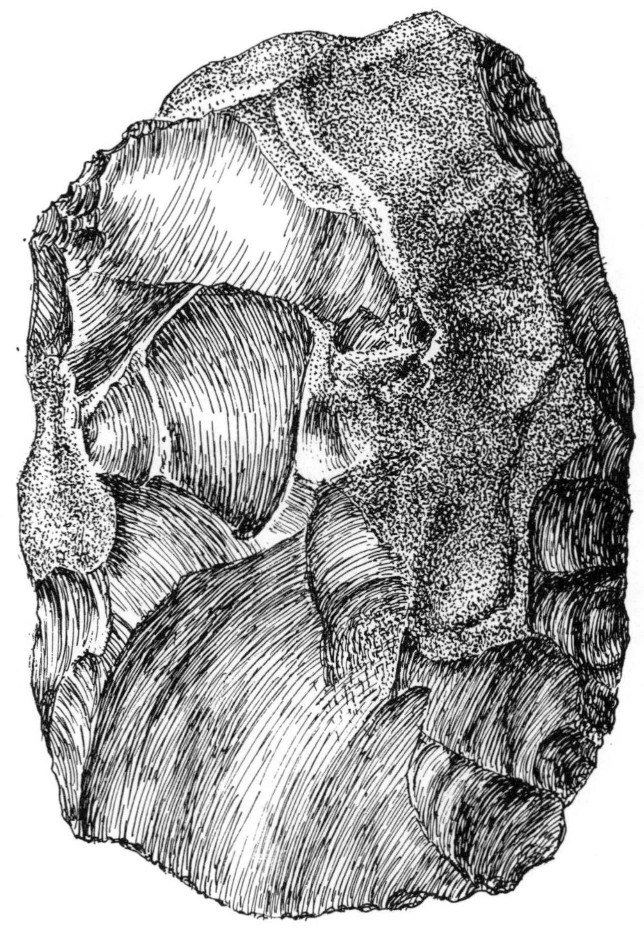

Above A small hand-axe from Swanscombe. *Right* A flint tool with a sharp cleaver edge from Swanscombe.

Man the Hunter

PEOPLE OF THE CAVE PERIOD

So passed tens of thousands of years, stretches of time impossible to imagine clearly. Then followed a phase of the Ice Age when conditions were so severe, with sheet-ice creeping over much of the country, that men and animals fled from Britain. Another warm period followed, during which men and animals returned and continued to live very much as before for several thousand years. Then came the last phase of the Ice Ages.

The final stage of the Ice Age, however, was not so severe as the earlier ones and there is plenty of evidence that Man lived in Britain at least for the greater part of it. But there was a different set of wild animals, fitted to seek food even under shallow snow. Such were the reindeer, the woolly rhinoceros and the heavily-furred, curved-tusked mammoth. Preying on them were meat-eating animals like the cave-lion and the hyaena. Man also joined the hunt and must have been constantly on the move, following the game herds, which supplied his food, and seeking out the cave-bear for its furry skin.

By now many implements were made of the relics of the chase – bone, ivory and antler; amongst these were spear-tips and harpoons, probably lashed to their hafts with animal sinews.

For the rest of their equipment men used what their ancestors discarded, that is the chips of flint which came off the central lumps In fact they so improved their craft that they were able to remove long sharp blades of flint, which could be used as knives or made into spear-tips, engraving tools and so forth.

At certain times of the year hunters had to find some kind of shelter from the cold. Maybe they made tents; certainly they had to make some kind of clothing and for these they must have used the skins of animals, which were sewn with beautiful needles made of bone.

In very severe weather these men and women sought shelter in caves and here we find the ashes of their fires, lit to keep away prowling animals as well as to give warmth. There is no evidence that they painted on the cave walls as their relations did on the Continent, but we do know that they could engrave bone and antler with pleasing designs.

Our picture is of a family at the mouth of Kent's Cavern in Devonshire; the woman is wearing skins and her husband is preparing a fire by rotating a hard stick against a piece of soft, dry wood.

Kent's Cavern, Devonshire. Making a fire.

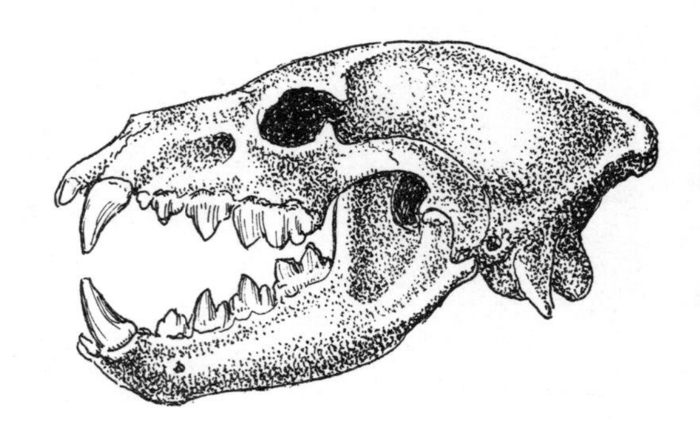

Above The skull of a hyaena. *Below* A bone needle and pin.

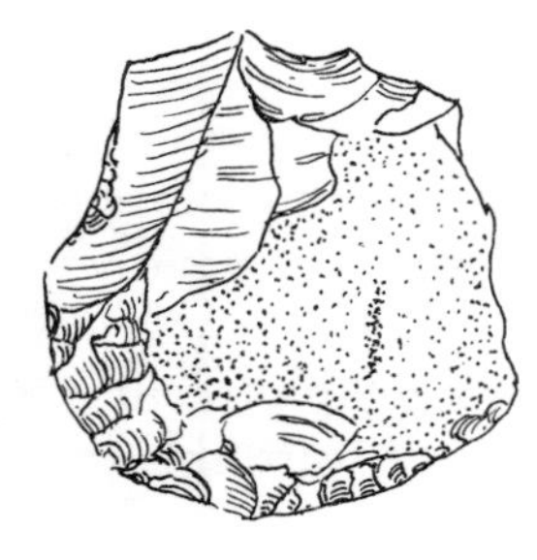

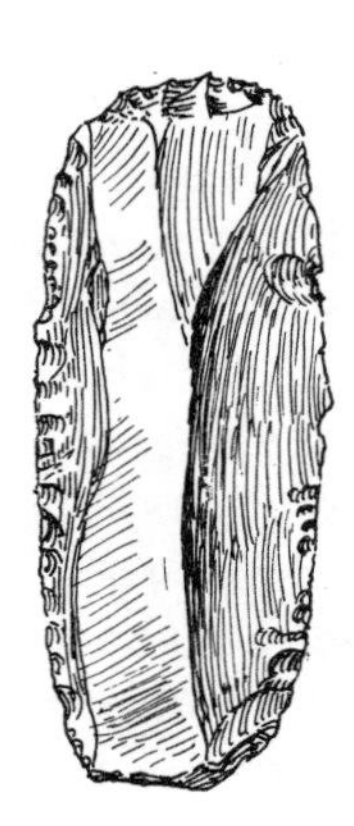

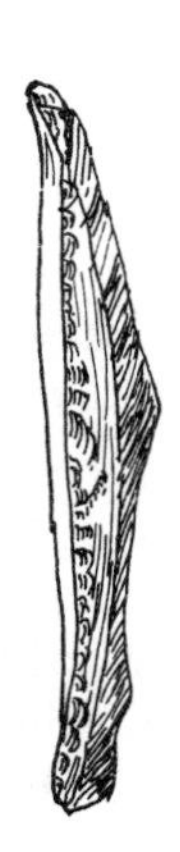

Above Flint scraper and blade possibly used for cleaning skins. *Below* The head of a harpoon carved from bone. The four subjects on these two pages are from Kent's Cavern, Devonshire.

Man the Hunter
THE END OF THE OLD STONE AGE

We must not think of the severe winters of the last part of the Ice Age as coming to an end quickly; several centuries passed before the climate really became noticeably warmer. Nor must we think of all Ancient Britons' way of life as changing very rapidly; changes, compared with changes today, were extremely slow.

The last of the people we think of as really belonging to the Old Stone Age probably continued to live very much as did their forefathers, but eventually they were able to live in somewhat more comfort. An over-hanging rock might provide a roof, and a wind-screen of branches and skins would serve to make a rough house.

Tools were still made mainly of flint, but the large number of knife-blades of this material suggests that their makers were able to use these to fashion finer articles of bone and wood for their use and comfort.

The largest of the game animals had moved away or become extinct and their place was taken by more deer and cattle, some of which were probably trapped or netted and some wounded and chased until they were exhausted, for there seem to have been no bows and arrows in Britain at this time.

The rock shelter in our picture is that at Creswell Crags in Derbyshire and this illustration shows the way in which skins were pegged out ready for drying and for scraping with flint tools.

Creswell Crags, Derbyshire. Pegging skin in a rock shelter.

Reindeer. Its antlers and bones were found shaped into tools at Creswell Crags, Derbyshire.

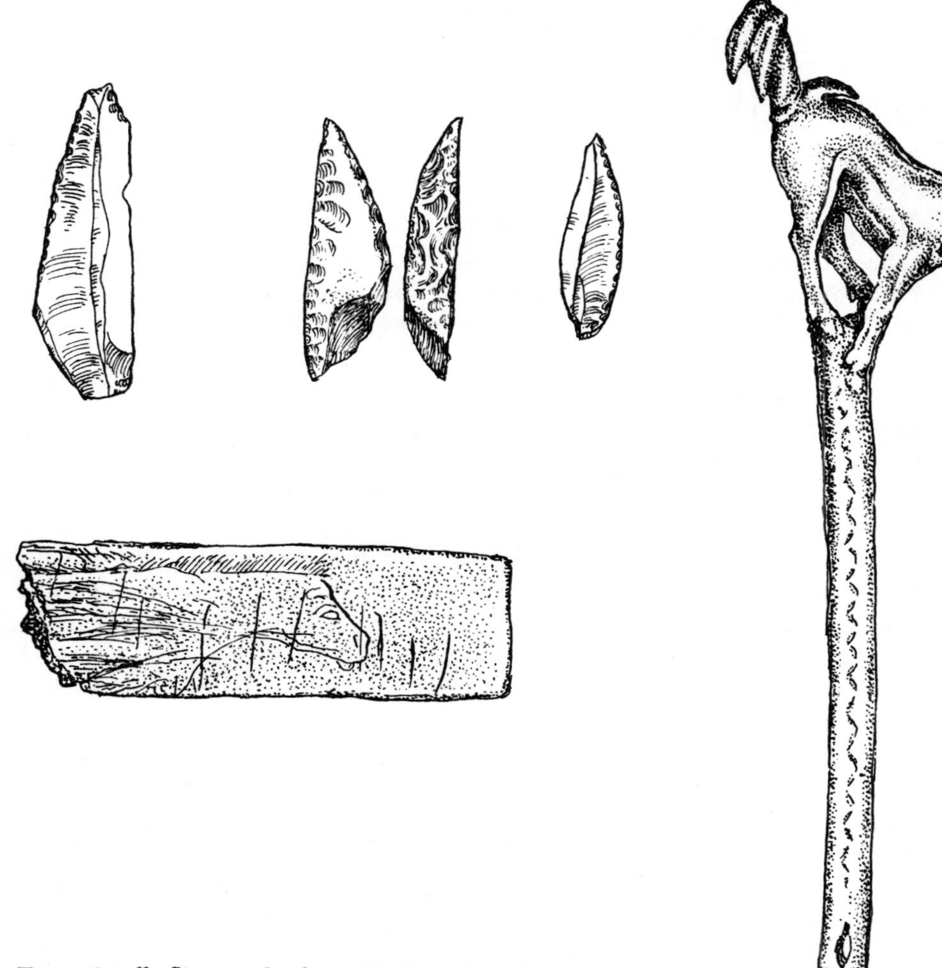

Top Small flint tools from Mother Grundy's Parlour, Derbyshire. *Centre* A fragment of bone with an engraving of a horse, from Creswell Crags. *Right* Carved antler spear-thrower from the cave of Mas d'Azil in Southern France.

Man the Hunter: Middle Stone Age

WATERSIDE LIFE

When the last of the glaciers of the Ice Age finally melted and the reindeer had retreated northwards, vegetation and trees gradually began to spread from the south to form a carpet of forest over the countryside, first of birches and pines and later of oaks, elms and beeches.

Men living in Britain at this time had adapted their way of life to new conditions. While there were elk, cattle and deer to be hunted, there were also great areas of marsh extending round the rivers and the coast – even across what is now the North Sea – and fishing offered a good supply of food.

Fish-hooks were made of bone and fish-traps of osier-twigs; antler and bone were also used for the making of barbed two-pronged eel- and fish-spears. The new growth of vegetation, however, made it difficult to move about in the damper areas. To cope with these conditions, people designed simple axes of flint for felling the smaller trees. Sometimes the boggy ground made it necessary to build platforms and jetties of felled timber. The remains of these have been found in the muddy peat which was left when the water gradually receded. On and near these platforms families would make their Summer camps and to them they brought the wild fowl and animals they had killed.

Amongst the other litter surrounding these camps have been found bones and antlers often cut and carved for the making of implements. Finer flint-work than had been attempted before was undertaken and very fine little points, blunted down the backs, were set into wooden shafts with resin.

In the picture an elk is being stalked by two hunters who have disguised themselves by wearing on their heads the antlers of deer that they have killed. The marshy ground is such as would be found at Star Carr in Yorkshire.

Opposite Star Carr, Yorkshire. Men of the Middle Stone Age hunting an elk. The stalkers wear deer antlers.

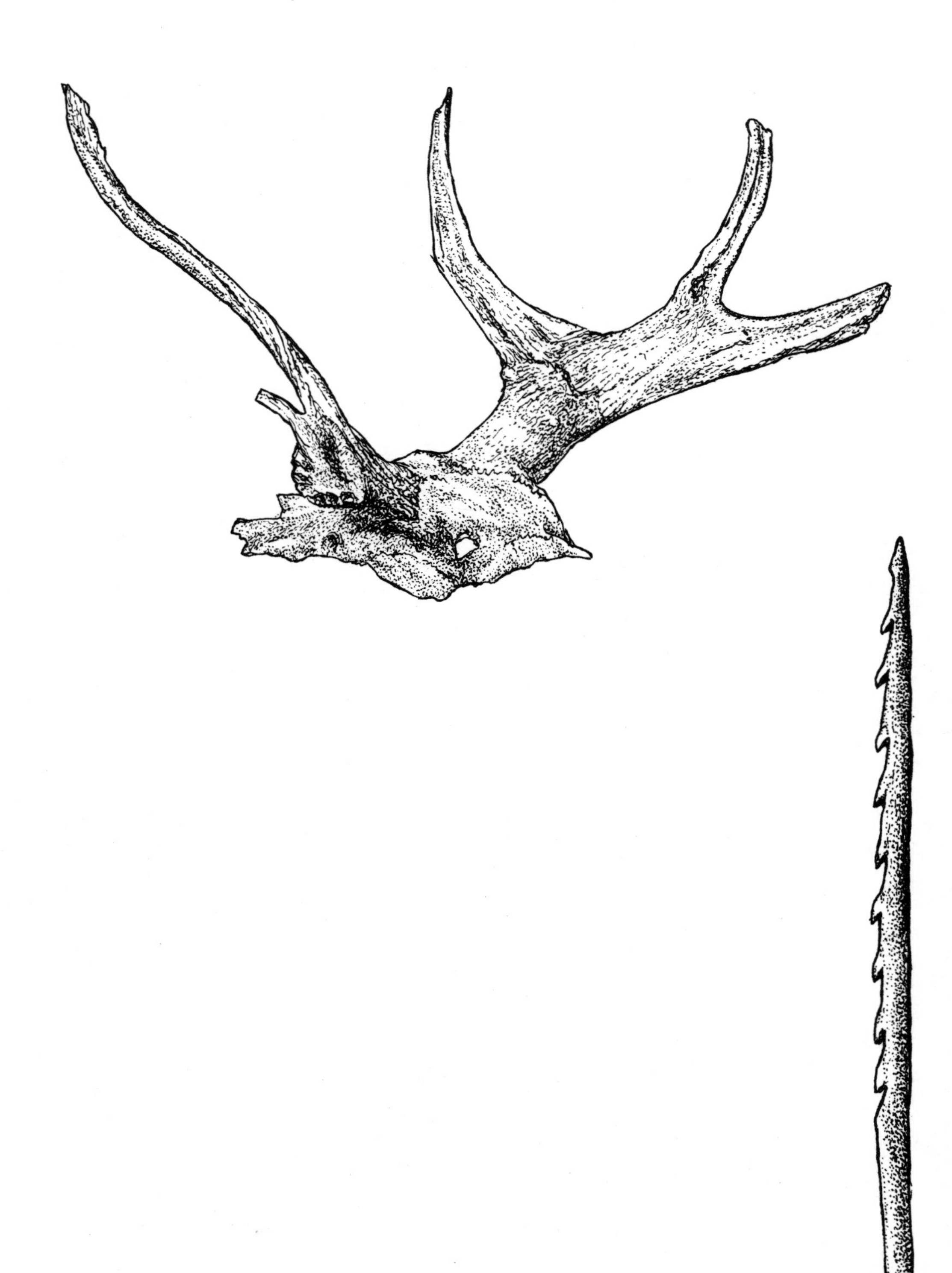

Above Deer antlers and part of the skull for the hunters' head-wear from Star Carr, Yorkshire. *Right* One prong from a forked fish-spear made of antler.

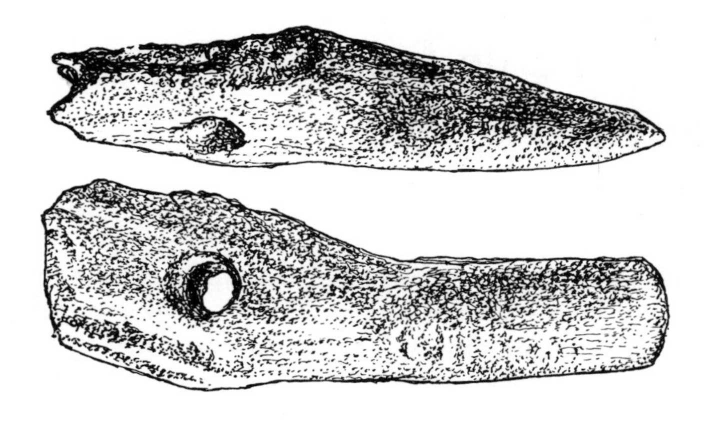

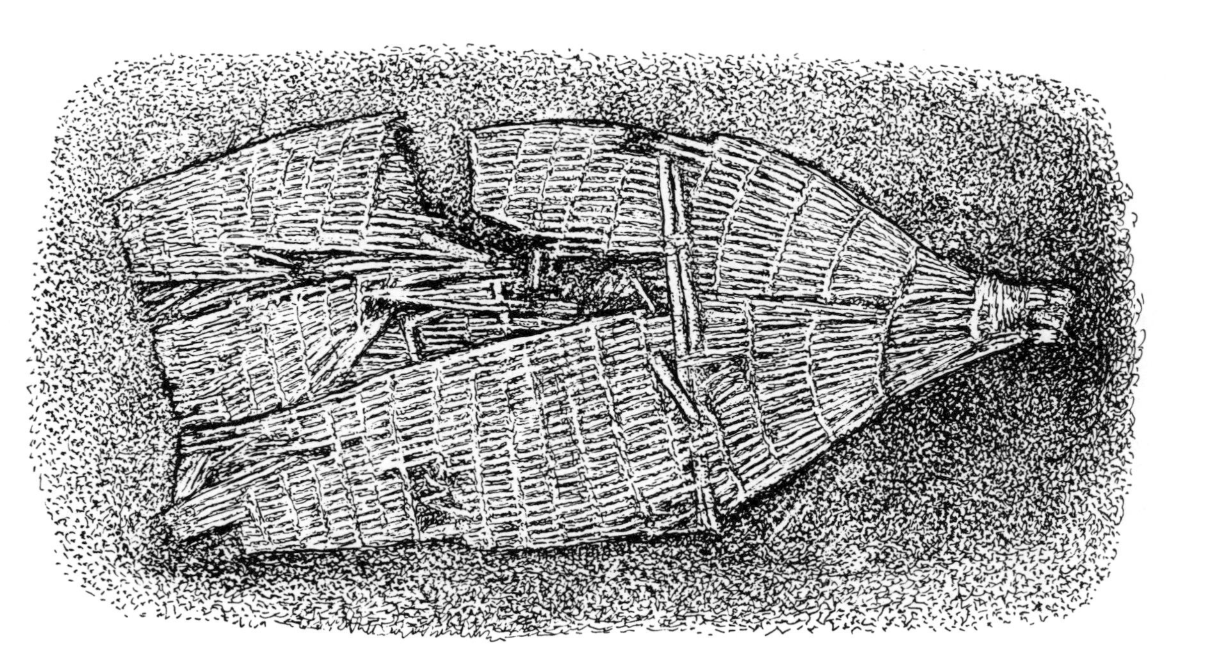

Above Two views of part of an elk antler drilled and shaped to form a mattock, probably used for digging. *Below* A fish-trap made of osiers, from a peat bog in Jutland, Denmark.

Man the Hunter: Middle Stone Age

HEATHLAND LIFE

While the Middle Stone Age fishers were living by water and marsh, other tribes lived and hunted on sandy soil and dry ridges where trees would not grow so thickly. Sometimes people lived high on hills, so avoiding swamps and forests. It is believed that they hunted deer and birds with bows and arrows, but no wood or bone survives in such conditions.

So many flint arrow-heads have been found that we may safely assume that these people did use arrows and bows. It seems likely, too, that sometimes several of the very tiny triangular and half-moon shaped flint blades these people made must have been set with resin in one shaft or handle to form a more complex tool.

In a few places slight hollows have been found surrounded by holes into which posts once fitted; these seem to be the remains of light huts, thatched with reeds and brush-wood. People must still have been constantly moving to find new sources of food and are unlikely to have had more permanent shelter.

Like hunters and trappers in other parts of the world today, these Middle Stone Age men must have lived partly by trading and, although they continued to live their own kind of life for some time after the farming peoples began to settle in Britain, they probably welcomed new people with whom they could trade and exchange.

This picture shows the kind of light brush-wood hut in which some men of the Middle Stone Age probably sheltered; traces of such a hut have been found at Abinger Hammer, Surrey. Skins were still used for clothing and the dog had become the companion of man in the chase – the first animal to be domesticated.

Horsham, Sussex. A hunter returning to his shelter with food.

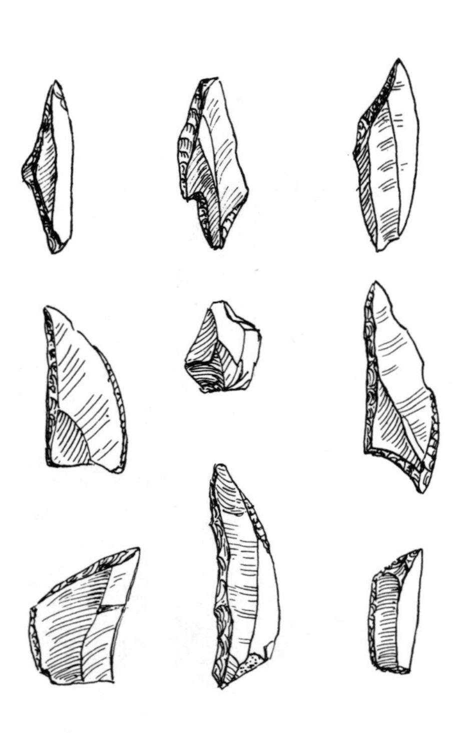

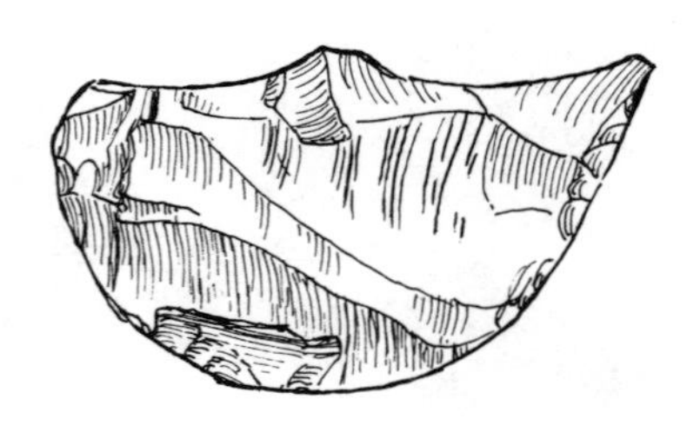

Left Middle Stone age small pointed flint tools finely chipped on some edges. Many were used as arrow heads. *Top right* A flint axe of which the sharp edge has been made by striking an oblique flake from the lower end. From Horsham, Sussex. *Below right* A typical flake removed from such an axe when re-sharpening.

Man the Farmer

FIRST CROPS AND HERDS

Men were still living by hunting, fishing and collecting wild fruits in Western Europe, but a new way of life was slowly being worked out in the warmer countries of the Near East. In the countries we now know as Iran, Iraq and Turkey men were learning to till the land and to sow the seeds of wild wheat and barley, reaping their crops and storing some of the grain for the following year's sowing. At the same time they were learning to tame wild cattle, sheep and goats so that their herds gave them milk, meat and hides without the need to be constantly on the move following wild game. These men were, in fact, the first farmers.

The idea of farming as a way of living spread slowly westwards into Europe until, about five thousand years ago, the first farmers arrived in Britain. They brought with them many other new ideas. Because they no longer had to be on the move, they were able to build larger and more permanent homes – though these were still very simple. Each hut was just a single rectangular room, usually with a fireplace at one end. The walls were low and made of stones and mud, while a thatched roof was held up by central timber posts. Each house was entered by a door at one end but there were probably no windows, and only a hole in the roof allowed smoke from the fire to escape. Although the huts were warm and dry inside they must have been very dark and smoky.

The cultivation of wheat and barley created two new activities in the home – the use of simple corn-mills and the making of pottery. The early type of mill was very simple but it was effective. The grain was placed in a slightly hollowed rough stone and was then ground into flour with a second, rounded, stone rubbed backwards and forwards. The flour was coarse and often contained a good deal of grit; as a result, the teeth of people who ate it quickly became worn. When we look at the teeth from the skeletons of people of this period we see that even young folk's teeth were badly worn.

Pottery for storing flour and pots for cooking were made in the home. Clay was dug and then mixed with sand. This mixture was rolled into lengths and, while still moist, one roll was coiled above another and the pot was thus built up. To make their surfaces smooth the pots were then rubbed all over with a rounded pebble; after which they were put in the sun or by the fireside to dry. Finally the pots were baked hard in a fire, and were then ready for use. The most common pot at this time was one with a rounded base as this would sit most easily on an open wood fire.

The two women in the foreground of the picture opposite are making pottery by coiling lengths of clay one upon another. In the background a third woman is busy grinding corn on a stone mill in front of a small house made of timber and thatch. The traces of such a house were found at Haldon in Devonshire.

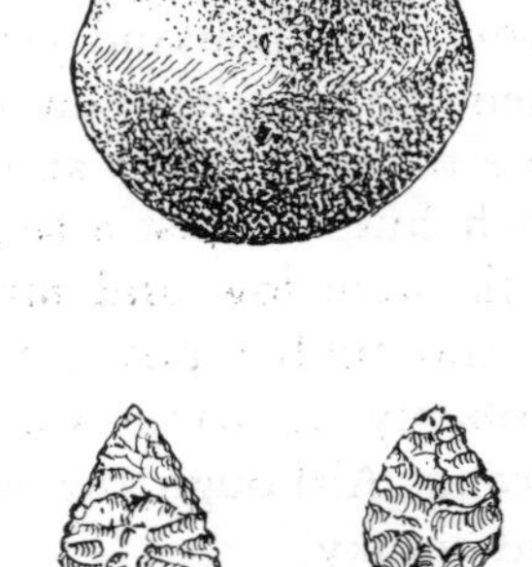

Top right The upper and lower stones of a mill for grinding corn, from Windmill Hill, Wiltshire. *Centre* A typical cooking pot with a round base, from Whitehawk Camp, Sussex. *Lower right* Two flint arrow-heads which are roughly leaf-shaped. They prove that the first farmers continued to hunt wild game. *Below* The impressions of a grain of wheat (*left*) made in the surface of a pot while it was still soft, before being fired. Similar impressions show that barley and flax were grown and that wild apples were being gathered; all from Windmill Hill, Wiltshire.

Opposite Haldon, Devonshire. Women making pots with coils of clay. In the background a woman grinds corn.

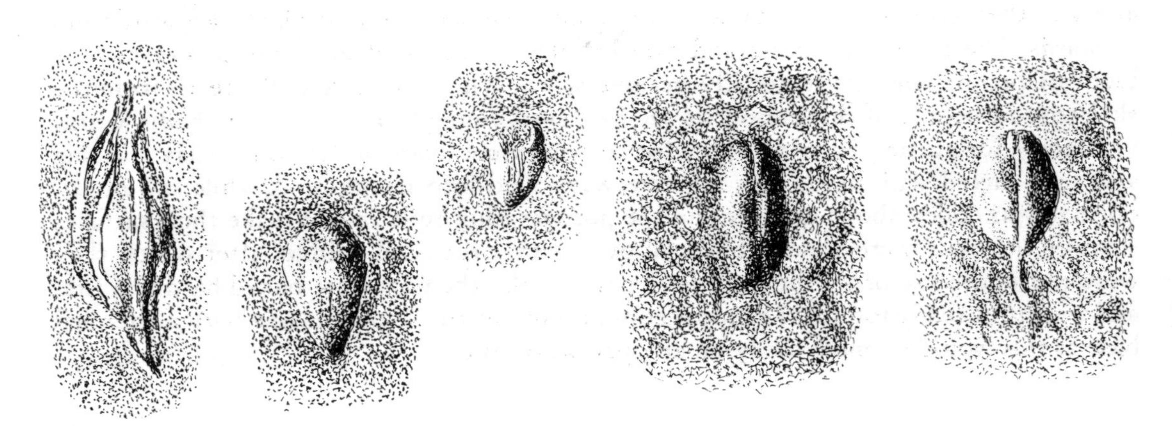

M·M·H.

Man the Farmer

THE FARMING SCENE

At this time most of the landscape of Europe was unlike that of today. Nearly all the land was covered either by forest or by marsh and before he could grow his crops man had to create fields. When a suitable piece of ground had been found the larger trees had to be felled with stone-bladed axes. The lighter timber and the undergrowth were then cut back and all the wood was burnt on the spot. This not only got rid of the wood but the ash fertilised the soil.

After a clearing in the forest had been made in this way, the soil was dug with wooden hoes or sharpened sticks and the grain could be sown. The crop was gathered by reaping the ears with small flint-bladed sickles, after which the stubble and weeds were burnt – as they still often are by farmers today – and the ground was made ready for the next crop. Growing the same crop in one field for very long exhausts the soil and so, after a few years, the early farmers had to leave their fields and make new ones by felling more trees. The old fields were not just allowed to become forest again: they were used for grazing sheep and cattle.

We think today of cattle as animals that live by eating grass, but the original wild cattle were forest dwellers. The early tamed cattle could be herded either in new clearings or in the forest itself, where they could eat leaves from shrubs or browse on the lower branches of trees. Sheep, on the other hand, originally came from mountain country and could do well only where there was natural grassland or moorland.

Because their feeding stuffs were rather poor, and because early man did not understand animal breeding, both sheep and cattle were thin and small; smaller in fact than their wild ancestors. The sheep especially were very different from those of today. Both ewes and rams had curling horns, and their fleeces, instead of being white and soft, had a good deal of hair amongst the wool and were of a dirty brown colour. A few sheep very much like this can still be seen on remote Scottish islands and, of course, in zoos.

Early farmers had one more important animal – the dog. As we have seen, the dog had been tamed and bred earlier by hunters to help in the chase. Now it took on a new task – helping to herd and protect the flocks from wild animals living in the forests: wolves, foxes and the larger birds of prey – for eagles were then to be found throughout our island

At the top of the hill in this picture one can see the ditches surrounding a meeting-place such as that at Windmill Hill in Wiltshire. An early farmer and his wife are reaping corn, the man using a flint-bladed sickle. The small sheep and cattle of this period can be seen browsing in the middle distance.

Windmill Hill, Wiltshire. Farming on the Downs: gathering grain and watching the herds.

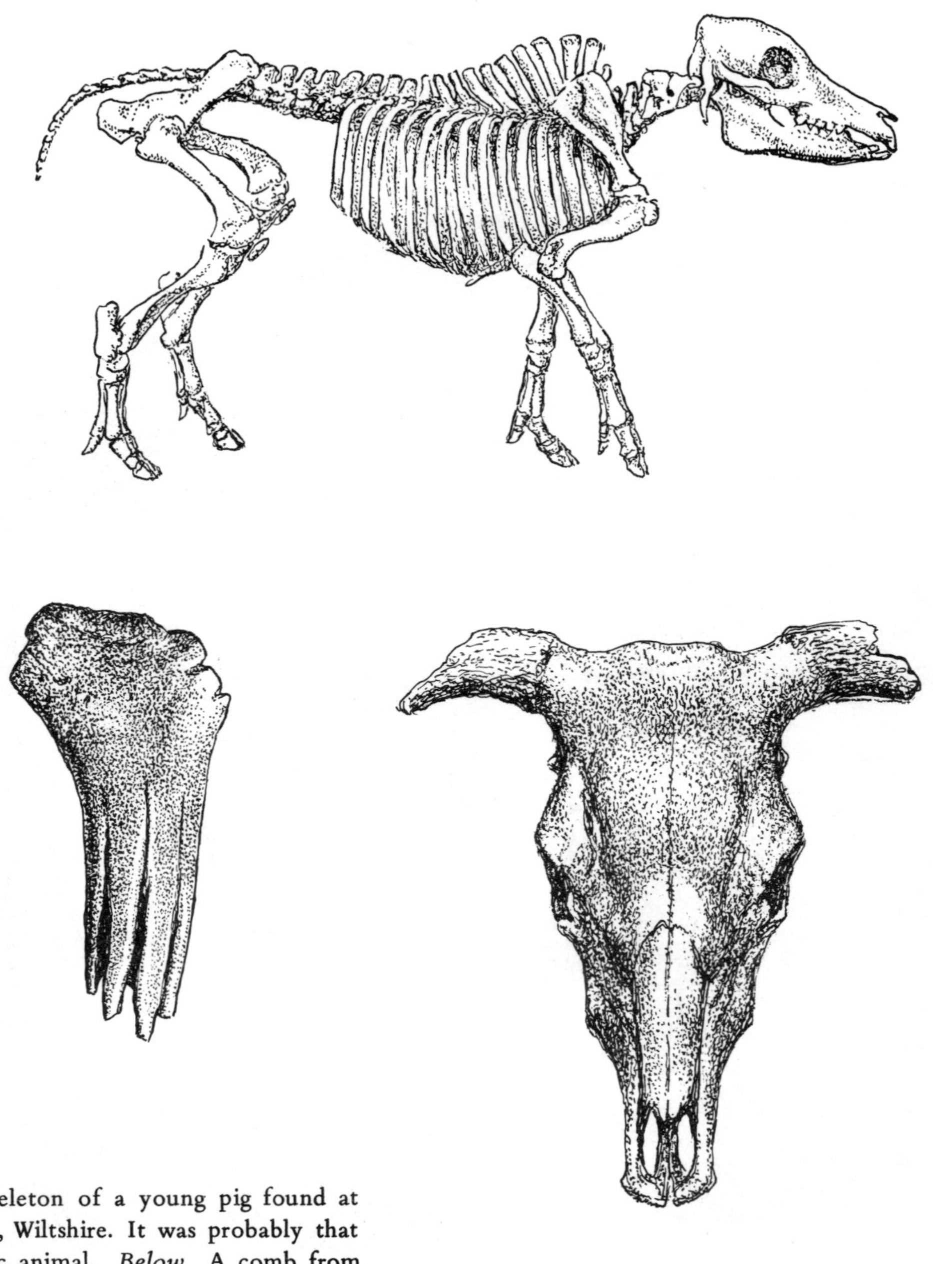

Top The skeleton of a young pig found at Windmill Hill, Wiltshire. It was probably that of a domestic animal. *Below* A comb from Windmill Hill made from a piece of deer antler. It was probably used to remove hair from skins when making leather. *Right* The skull of a small domestic ox.

Man the Farmer

MINING FOR FLINT

Just as in the Old and Middle Stone Ages men used flint for making many of their tools, so in the New Stone Age this material was needed for the same purposes. But now tools were, on the whole, made far more carefully – even beautifully – often being trimmed to precise shapes. In order that this could be done only the best quality flint, which would flake exactly as the tool-maker wanted, could be used. Flint that has been exposed to the weather often has fine cracks in it and so lumps of flint gathered from the surface of the ground were not always reliable. To get over this difficulty men of the New Stone Age learned how to mine for good uncracked flint.

Flint is found almost everywhere in chalk. It exists as bands of irregularly-shaped lumps between layers of chalk. In order to get at the flint miners had to dig the shafts downwards through the chalk with picks and shovels.

The antlers of red deer provided the picks, for by cutting away most of the points, or tines, the miners had an ideal tool: the main beam of the antler served as a handle and the remaining tine as the pointed tip with which the chalk was levered out. The flat, triangular shoulder-blade bones of cattle were fitted with wooden handles and used as shovels. The waste chalk and flint lumps were loaded into bags or baskets and carried or hauled to the top of the shaft.

Often the miners dug down through some layers of flint because they produced only poor material. When they reached a good band they dug along sideways so making caves and tunnels reaching away from the pit-shaft. In these tunnels it was often too dark to work without light of some kind and the miners had to use lamps; these they made by hollowing out lumps of chalk so that they would hold some animal fat in which floated a wick of reed or moss.

With their few simple tools miners were able to bring lumps of flint to the surface where they were broken into convenient pieces. The pieces were then roughly chipped into something like the shape of an axe; in the final stage these rough-outs were often ground and polished, probably with wet sand.

Flint, of course, was also used for making smaller sharp implements. In this case the lumps would be trimmed into carefully prepared shapes and then fine blades could be struck off them.

The blades were then trimmed and flaked to provide beautifully finished implements, arrow-heads and knives; their surfaces are usually covered with a mass of fine chip-scars giving the appearance of the rippled surface of water.

The miners in the picture have prised out lumps of flint, with picks made of deer-antler, from chalk in the passages that can be seen in the background. They have brought the flint to the foot of their shaft and it is being hoisted in skin bags to the surface.

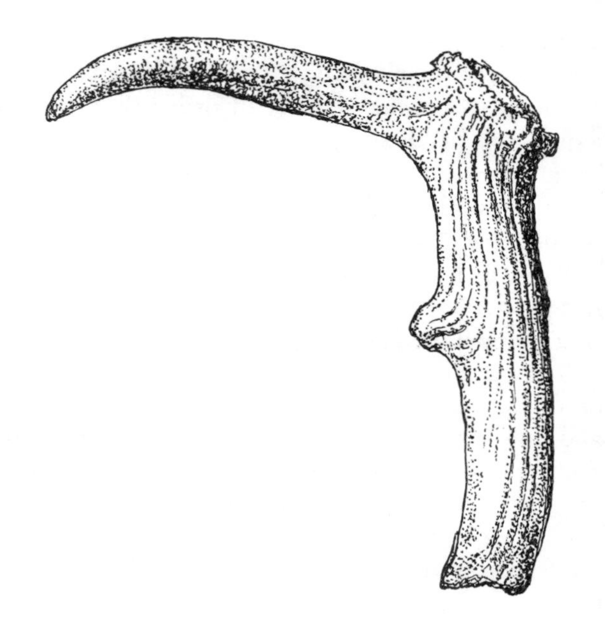

Right **In the flint mines at Grimes' Graves, Norfolk, there were found many miners' picks such as this.** ***Below*** **A shovel made from the shoulder-blade of an ox. The handle is of antler.**

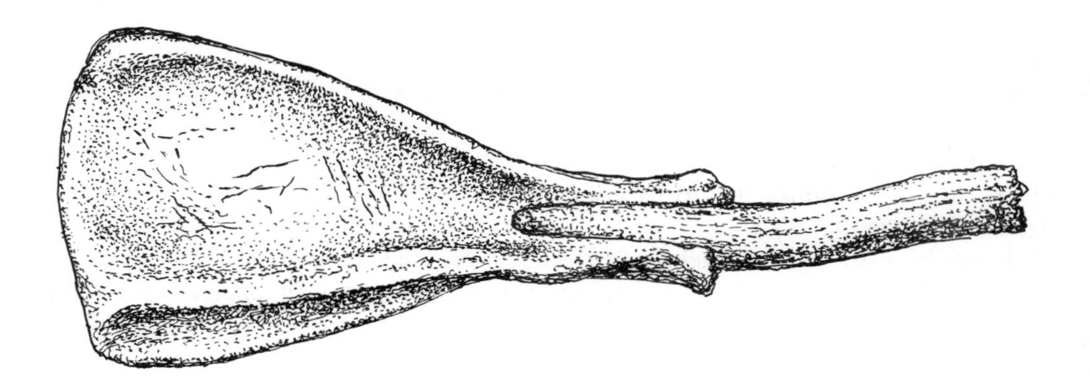

Grimes' Graves, Norfolk. Man learns to mine for flint.

Man the Farmer

STONE AXE-HEADS

So much of the early farmer's activity depended upon his being able to fell trees and to work timber that there was a constant demand for stone axe-blades. Flint was available on parts of the chalk-lands but the type of rock that made really good, tough blades was not to be found everywhere. In time a number of suitable outcrops of rock were discovered and an industry grew up with people specialising in quarrying and in trading in axe-heads.

When suitable stone was discovered it was quarried by splitting pieces from the rock-face by driving wooden wedges into natural cracks. Sometimes a fire was lit against the face so as to heat it; it was then suddenly doused with cold water with the result that the sudden cooling made the rock crack. The quarried lumps were broken into smaller pieces and these were trimmed by flaking roughly into the shape of axes.

It was in the form of unfinished rough-outs that the stone was carried across country, the buyers doing the slow work of finally shaping and polishing them into usable axe-heads. After polishing, axe-heads of this time were most commonly fixed to a wooden shaft with a binding, but if a shaft-hole in the axe-head was wanted it had to be drilled. This was done with a bone-tipped drill, sand and water being poured round the drill-head as it turned – the water for cooling and the sand to do the cutting. It was a slow process and drill-points must have worn down rapidly, but the result was a neat straight-sided shaft-hole.

Stone axe-heads were traded far afield; for example some heads found in Kent are known to have come originally from quarries in the hills of South Wales. We know this because the different rocks used in axe-making are made up of different minerals. By cutting a thin slice out of an axe we can examine these minerals under a microscope and, when this has been done, it is possible to find out in what part of the country the rock is to be found. Actual quarries have been discovered; in fact we know of about two dozen such quarries used in this period – most of them in the north of England, Wales and Cornwall.

In this picture two men are quarrying rock for axe-heads at the Pike O'Stickle, Cumberland. A lump of rock has been heated and is being doused with water by one of the men; the other is about to break it by hitting it with a large boulder.

Pike O'Stickle, Cumberland. Splitting rocks to make tools.

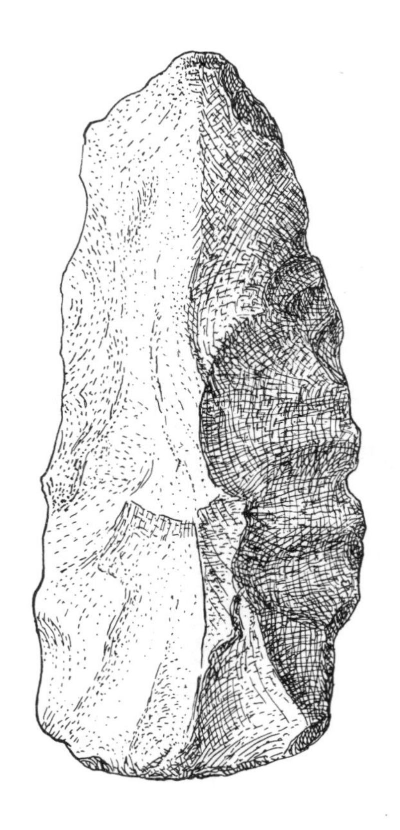

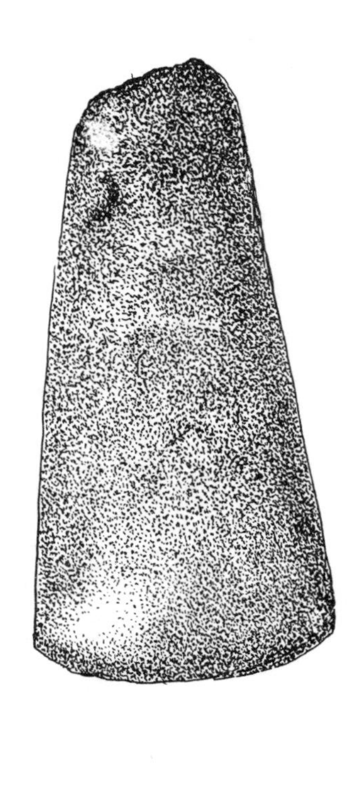

Above left A piece of stone roughly shaped into the form of an axe-head, from Pike O'Stickle, and *(right)* a finished axe after polishing, found at Shapwick Heath, Somerset. The stone came from North Wales. *Right* A hammer-stone from Pike O'Stickle.

The Pike O'Stickle as it is today. Suitable stone for making axes was only to be found in the hard rocks of hilly country.

Man the Farmer

LIVING BY WATER

In a country covered with thick forest, getting about was something of a problem for, although there were probably a few tracks and pathways leading from one group of dwellings to another, there was nothing like a road. To travel long distances people had either to follow rivers along their banks on foot or go by boat.

Some boats were possibly made by stretching skins over light wooden frames, but frail craft of this kind have not survived. More solid boats were made by hollowing out large tree-trunks. A suitable tree, usually an oak, was felled, the bark removed and the branches cut away. The trunk was then fired and, as the wood charred, it was chipped away. Slowly the trunk was hollowed out in this way to make a canoe.

Boats of this kind had one great disadvantage; if they were allowed to become dry they would split and so they always had to be kept damp. When people left their boats for a time they sank them in water to make sure that they would not become dry. Sometimes the owners of the boats never did return and, in time, the canoe sank deeper and deeper into the muddy bottom of the river or lake. Since deep wet mud prevents wood from rotting, boats of this kind are found today – and quite well preserved.

Although the early farmers usually chose to settle in upland areas where the forest was not thick some people chose dwelling places on the banks of lakes and wide rivers. Having canoes they could get about easily and they could always add to their food supply by fishing and killing water-birds.

From our point of view the lake-side dwellings are very valuable, for, exactly as with the canoes, wooden objects that would have perished elsewhere have been preserved in the damp mud. From this kind of dwelling there have been removed, still in quite good condition, such things as canoe paddles, bows, arrows, stone axes with their wooden hafts and a wide range of household goods like wooden bowls and baskets. But for these finds it would be very difficult to know what tools and other equipment these people used.

The men in this picture are hollowing out a tree-trunk to make a canoe. One man is fanning a fire to burn the wood while the other is chipping away the charred wood. Boats like this must have been used, for example, at Ehenside Tarn in Cumberland.

Ehenside Tarn, Cumberland. Making a dug-out canoe

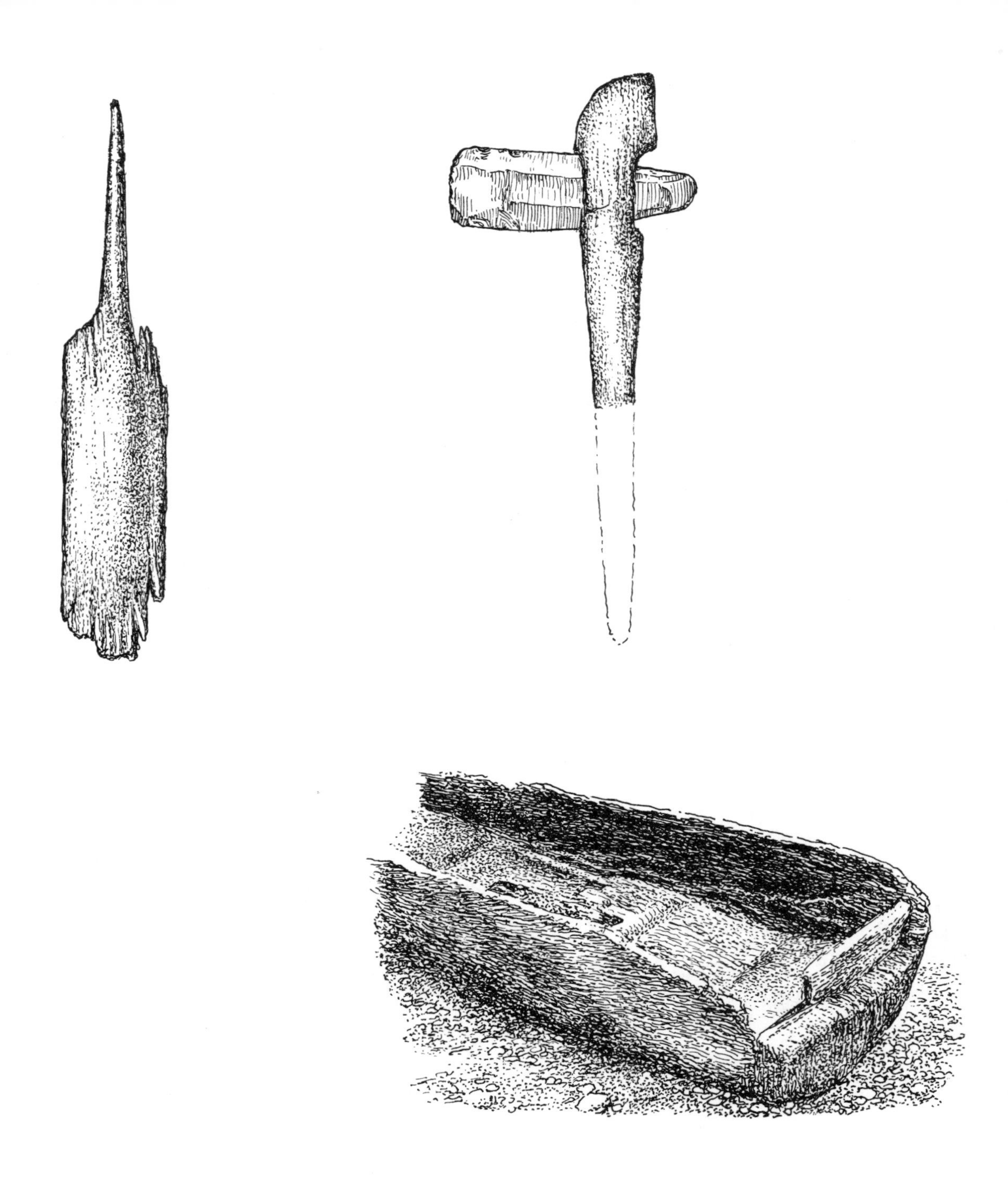

Above left Remains of a wooden canoe paddle from Ehenside Tarn, Cumberland. *Above right* The upper part of the wooden handle of this axe from Ehenside Tarn was well preserved in the lake mud. The blade is of stone. *Below* The stern end of a dug-out canoe from the River Trent, Nottinghamshire. The end has probably been repaired by letting a board into a slot.

Man the Farmer

HOUSES OF THE DEAD

Although the houses of the early farmers were small and simple and their tools primitive, they were able to make large stone and earth structures. They went to quite extraordinary lengths to prepare what they thought were proper burying places for their dead. Their long burial-mounds – or long barrows – sometimes a hundred yards or more in length, remain as a common feature of our present countryside; they may be seen especially near the tops of hills.

The burial customs of the time seem strange to us now, although there are many primitive peoples who still treat their dead in much the same way. The bodies were not buried straightaway but were placed in wooden houses, where they were left for a long time and until only the bones remained; then the final burial was prepared.

In places where there was plenty of rock a stone chamber was built, but in other areas the chamber had to be of wood. The bones were taken from the temporary house of the dead and carefully laid to rest in the new chamber; then a mound of stones or earth was built over it. In the case of earthen mounds, or barrows, the soil was dug from two ditches, one on each side of the mound. Finally, the entrance of the chamber was blocked and covered with soil or stones.

What led people to bury the dead in this way will probably never be known, but several points do appear to be clear. Usually in front of the entrance to the chamber there is a small courtyard and here the last rites must have been performed. It seems, too, that usually the bones from several different bodies were all placed in the chamber at the same time; so the ceremonies may have taken place only when someone very important, such as a tribal chief, died and had to be buried. Or perhaps there was a burial ceremony only at special times or every so many years.

Burial mounds were not the only large and complicated structures made by these early farmers. They also built special meeting places and these, too, are usually found on the tops of hills. A roughly circular area was marked out by a number of short lengths of ditch, sometimes in such a way that they made a single interrupted ring; but more often they were arranged to form two or three interrupted rings one inside the other, as can be seen in the picture on page 31.

In these places the people of the tribe gathered for some kind of ceremony or festival at which there would be singing, dancing and feasting. Possibly they gathered also for more serious business, such as the settlement of arguments, the making of laws, the discussion of tribal business and the exchange of goods, but these are all matters about which we can only guess, since all that has been left for us to discover are the meat-bones from their meals and a few scraps of broken pottery in the ditches.

As our picture shows, large numbers of people must have worked together to set up the huge stones of which the central burial chambers (such as those in the long barrow at Notgrove, Gloucestershire) were constructed. Ropes, levers and wooden rollers were probably used to move the stones.

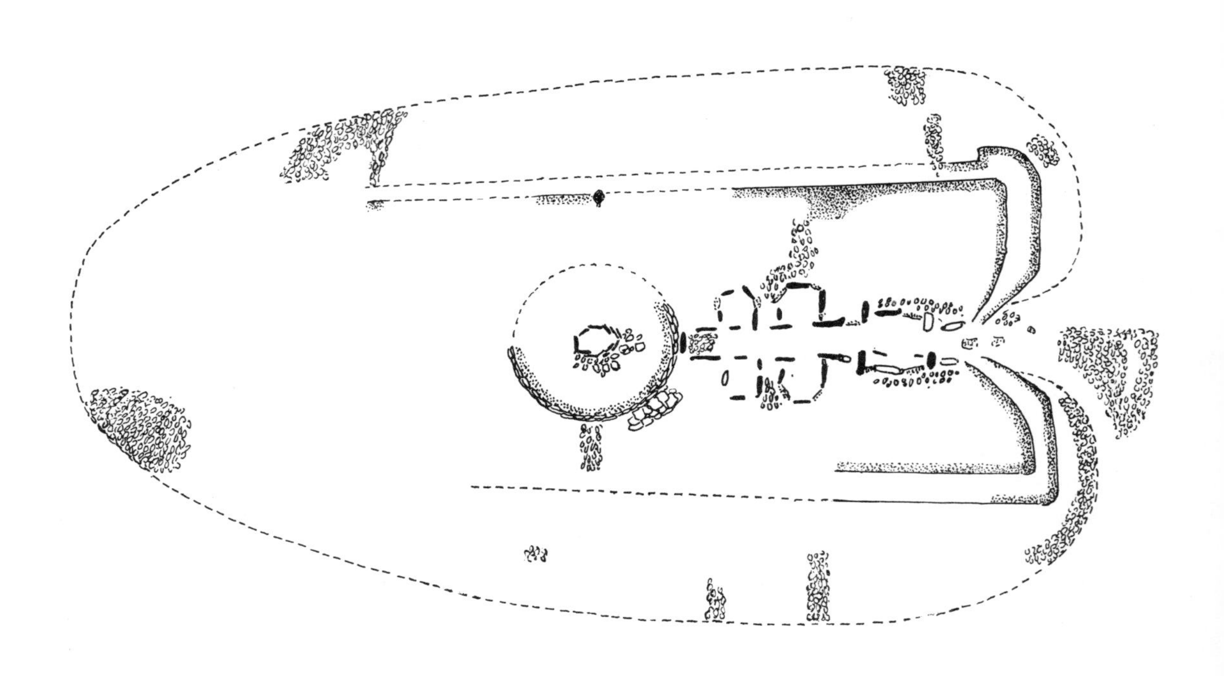

A plan of the long barrow at Notgrove, Gloucestershire, showing an entrance on the right leading to a number of stone-lined chambers.

Notgrove, Gloucestershire. Constructing a Long Barrow.

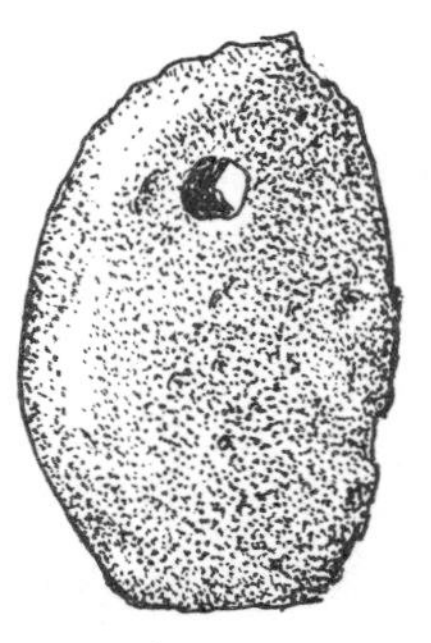

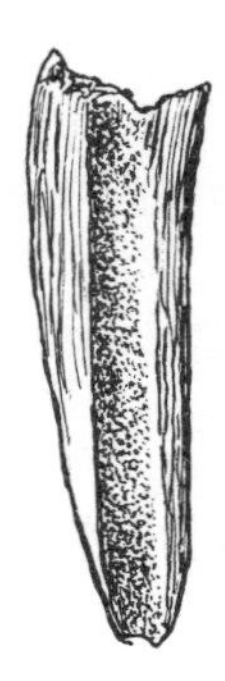

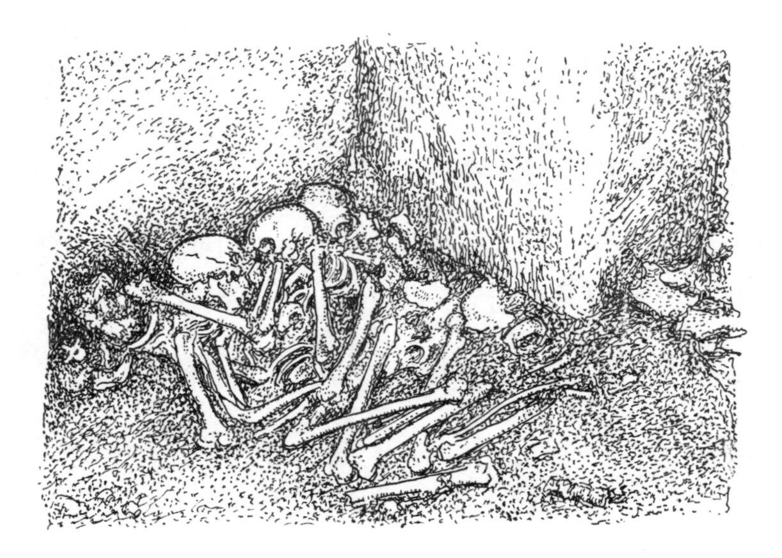

Above left Bored stone from Notgrove, and (*right*) a horse tooth used as a gouge, also from Notgrove. *Below* Human skeletons found in a chamber of the long barrow at West Kennet, Wiltshire.

The Coming of Metals

THE SEARCH FOR GOLD AND COPPER

As with the idea of farming, so the discovery that metals could be shaped into tools and ornaments was made not in Europe but in the Near East. The first metal to be used was gold, largely because it occurs naturally as a bright, shiny metal and it can be hammered easily into shape. Gold is found in thin layers running through rocks, but wind, rain and frost break up the rocks in time and the gold is then carried away in small pieces by water to the stream valleys. Gold is very heavy and the large pieces are not carried far; they settle down amongst the lighter particles of sand and gravel in the stream bed.

The way in which gold was panned or separated from sand and gravel was very simple. The sand, with the gold in it, was scooped up and put with water in a flat open pan. Then the pan was shaken in such a way that the water swirled round and slopped over the edges of the pan, carrying the lighter sand with it; the heavier fragments of gold were left in the bottom of the pan. In this way enough gold was collected to allow early metal-workers to hammer the fragments together and to make small ornaments.

Of course not every river valley produces gold. Indeed there were very few in Britain – chiefly in Cornwall, Wales, Scotland and Ireland. Nevertheless, there was enough of the precious metal to attract goldsmiths from other parts of Europe, already skilled in the arts of searching for and shaping it.

Gold ornaments, like ear-rings and neck-bands, were made by beating the metal into thin sheets and then trimming them into shape, and the metal was soft enough to be worked with only stone, bone and flint tools.

A second metal whose use was taught to the people of Western Europe at much the same time was copper. This was seldom found naturally as a metal; it was usually found combined with other substances in the form of bright blue and green rocks. It was removed by heating the rocks in a very hot fire. When this was done the copper became molten and could be run into hollows cut into pieces of stone where, on cooling, it set solid in these simple moulds. The rough copper shapes could then be hammered and finally polished to form knives, axe-heads and simple tools.

Although copper tools were in most ways better than the stone and flint ones, they must have been expensive to make and only chieftains would have been able to command them. Lesser folk still had to make do with stone tools and, while the chieftains decked themselves with gold, more ordinary people went on using beads of bone and stone.

In the picture the older man on the left is swirling round a pan containing sand from the bed of a mountain stream and the younger man is adding more sand and water from time to time. In time enough gold will gather in the bottom of the pan to be worth collecting.

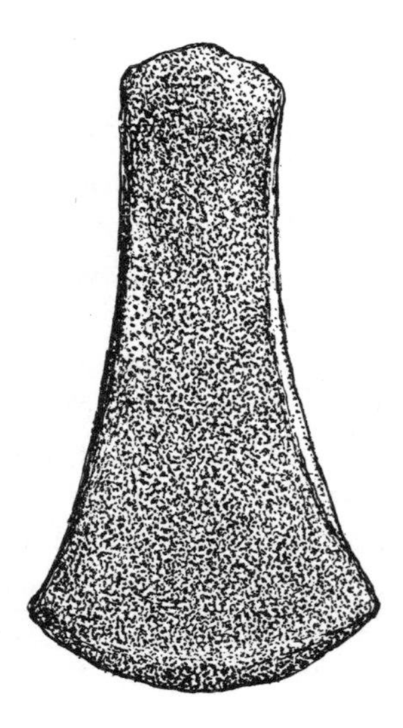

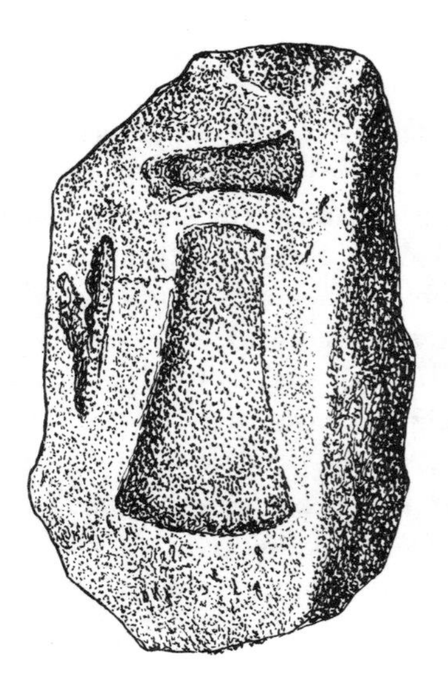

Above left A copper axe from Migdale, Sutherland, such as could have been made in the stone mould on the right. The mould was for a copper flat axe, from Dufftown. *Left* A drinking cup or beaker from Dorchester. The shape, rather like an inverted bell, is typical of this type of cup.

Lor, Cornwall, Panning for gold.

Right Basket earrings found in a young man's grave. *Below* A neck ornament made from a sheet of gold. The decoration on the ornament would have been made by using copper or flint punches. It was found in Co. Kerry, Ireland.

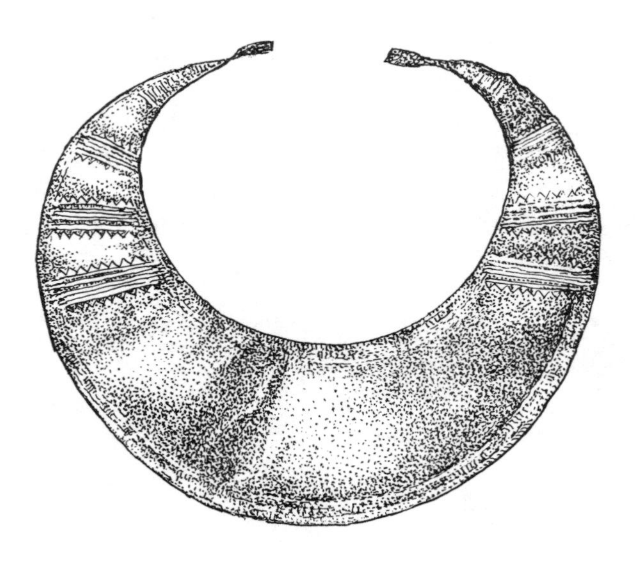

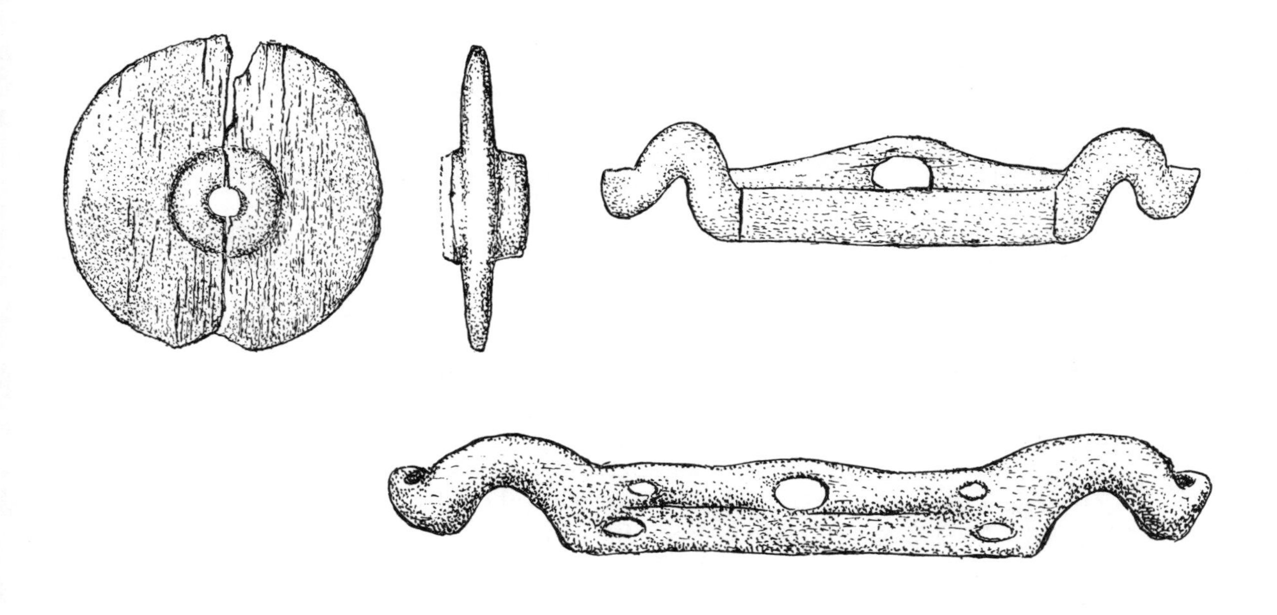

Above left A cart wheel made of a single piece of wood, dug up in a peat bog in Holland, and *(right)* a wooden ox-yoke found in a peat bog in Ireland. We are not certain of its age, but it is very similar to yokes still in use in Turkey today, *(underneath)* a horse-yoke from Ireland. *Below* A view of a wooden roadway for waggons near Glastonbury, Somerset, as it probably was when in use. Much of the wood was preserved in the peat bog in which it was later submerged.

The Coming of Metals

WAGONS AND INVADERS

Something else which was new to Britain reached our shores at about this time. Quite recently archaeologists have discovered a wooden trackway crossing the marshes in Somerset. This, they have been able to show, is of about the same age as the earliest copper tools. This primitive road made of logs and brushwood held in place by posts and pegs, is so wide that it seems it must have been designed to allow wagons to pass along it. Unfortunately no remains of these early carts have been found in Britain, but in Holland a number of wooden wheels of the same age, cut from a single solid piece of oak, have been dug up in the peat-bogs in which they have been preserved.

Of course we cannot be absolutely sure what these wagons looked like, but we do know that the first carts were invented, like so many other things, in the Near East, and in some parts of Europe clay models – probably toys – have been discovered as well as models of the oxen which pulled them.

So we have at least some idea of their appearance. The pair of oxen carried a wooden yoke over their shoulders; to the middle of this was attached a pole, the other end of which was fixed to the wagon. The wagon itself was a simple wooden platform with a pair of axles on which four wheels turned, while the sides of the cart were made by setting a number of upright stakes into holes cut into the platform.

Ox-drawn carts, although slow and awkward, did allow people to move heavy loads more easily and, if they wished, to pack up all their belongings and move somewhere else. In fact, the first appearance in Britain of both metals and carts came at the same time as the arrival of a new people, who seem to have been far more given to moving about than the early farmers. Perhaps this was because they had large flocks and herds and had to be constantly on the move in search of fresh pastures.

These invaders are known to archaeologists as the Beaker People because they chose to be buried with a drinking vessel of a particular kind. They were often buried with knives, stone-headed axes and bows and arrows, so that we may guess that they were rather war-like in contrast to the early farmers. Indeed they over-ran a large part of Central and Western Europe as well as Britain. At first they must have caused great alarm by stealing much of their land from the early farmers, but in time the invaders and the earlier inhabitants married, to found a new and quite different pattern of living, with a blend of old and new ideas.

The cart pulled by oxen in the picture is based on models found in other parts of Europe and upon existing carts still in use today in Turkey. Coming over the brow of the small hill is a party of armed raiders.

The Somerset Levels. The arrival of the Beaker Folk.

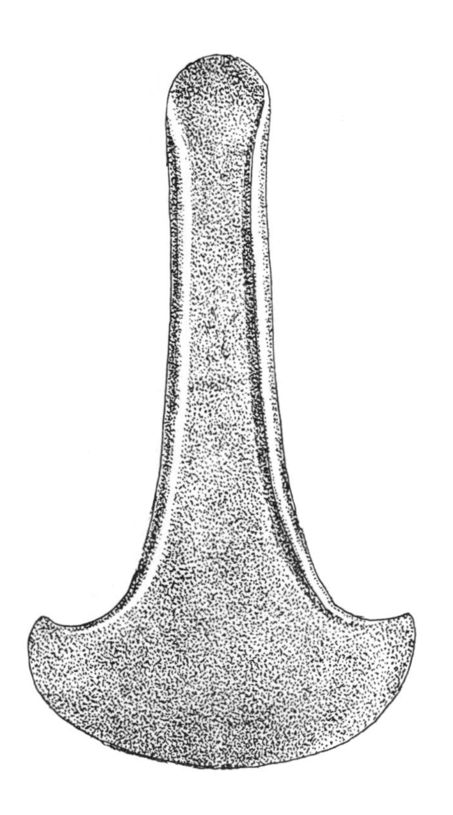

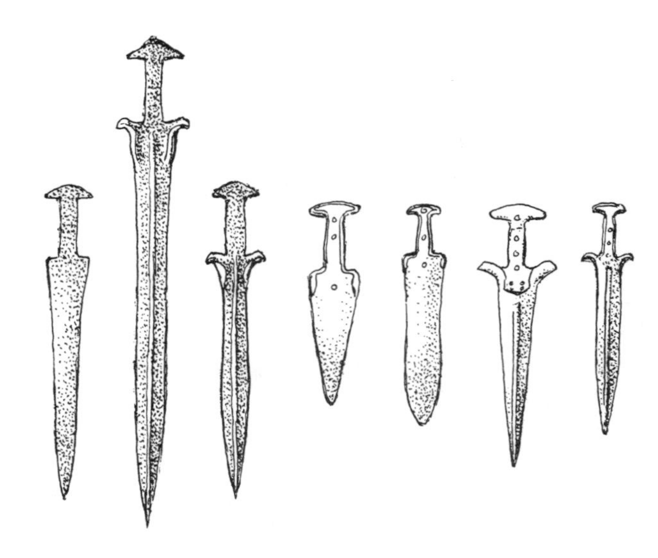

Top Engravings of axe-heads and a dagger of bronze on one of the upright stones at Stonehenge. *Above* Swords and daggers found in Crete of the same age as those at Stonehenge. Notice the similarity of their shape to that in the engravings at Stonehenge. *Left* An axe-head from Arreton Down, Wiltshire, the same shape as those engraved.

The Coming of Metals

STONEHENGE

Stonehenge, standing in the middle of Salisbury Plain, is one of the most extraordinary structures ever to be built by a primitive people. The place was clearly some kind of a temple, probably set up by men who worshipped the sun, and, although there are many other circles of upright stones in Britain, all of which were built at about the same period, Stonehenge is quite unique for two important reasons.

First, standing stones were usually obtained locally, but, in the case of Stonehenge, some of the smaller stones – which, even so, weigh many hundredweights – were brought to the middle of what is now England from the mountains of South Wales. This in itself was a fantastic feat. The great lumps of rock were probably moved on sledges to the south coast of Wales and there put onto barges and brought up the Severn Estuary. From the Bristol Avon the stones were moved, partly by raft on the rivers, partly by sledge over land, to their present position.

The second great difference between Stonehenge and other stone circles lies in the fact that the great upright stones with their ring of cap-stones were all carefully shaped into neat rectangular blocks, whilst elsewhere the stones were left in the rough forms in which they were found. Furthermore, during the trimming, two knobs were left on the top of each upright stone, which fitted into cup-shaped hollows cut into the cap-stones. As a final refinement, each cap-stone is slightly curved to make up part of a great circle.

There can be no doubt that the upright stones were set up by digging a hole in the ground, sliding the bottom end of the stone over it and then levering the stone up with long wooden poles so that it slid by gravity into position.

The lintels or cap-stones were probably raised by levering up first one end and then the other and sliding a wooden wedge underneath on each occasion. By repeating this operation a crude wooden scaffolding was made which, when tall enough, would allow the lintel to be worked into position.

It seems almost impossible that the early people of Britain can have managed this great feat of engineering without outside help and we cannot help wondering if the whole work was not managed by someone who already knew something of this kind of building. In fact we have a small but important clue.

On one of the upright stones a number of shapes have been cut into the face of the rock. Most of them we can recognise as the outlines of simple metal axe-heads, but one of them is distinctly the outline of a dagger; and it is of a shape unknown in Britain but quite common at the time on the Island of Crete. What is more, we know that the Cretans were adventurous seamen, who certainly travelled the whole length of the Mediterranean in a search for metals, and that they built tombs and temples from large blocks of trimmed stone in their own island. On the face of things it seems possible that some early merchant-venturer may have added his knowledge to the building of Stonehenge.

The builders to be seen in the foreground of our picture have raised one of the curved cap-stones as we have just described and will soon be able to work it into position on the uprights. Another group of men on the far side of the stone circle is just beginning to raise a second cap-stone.

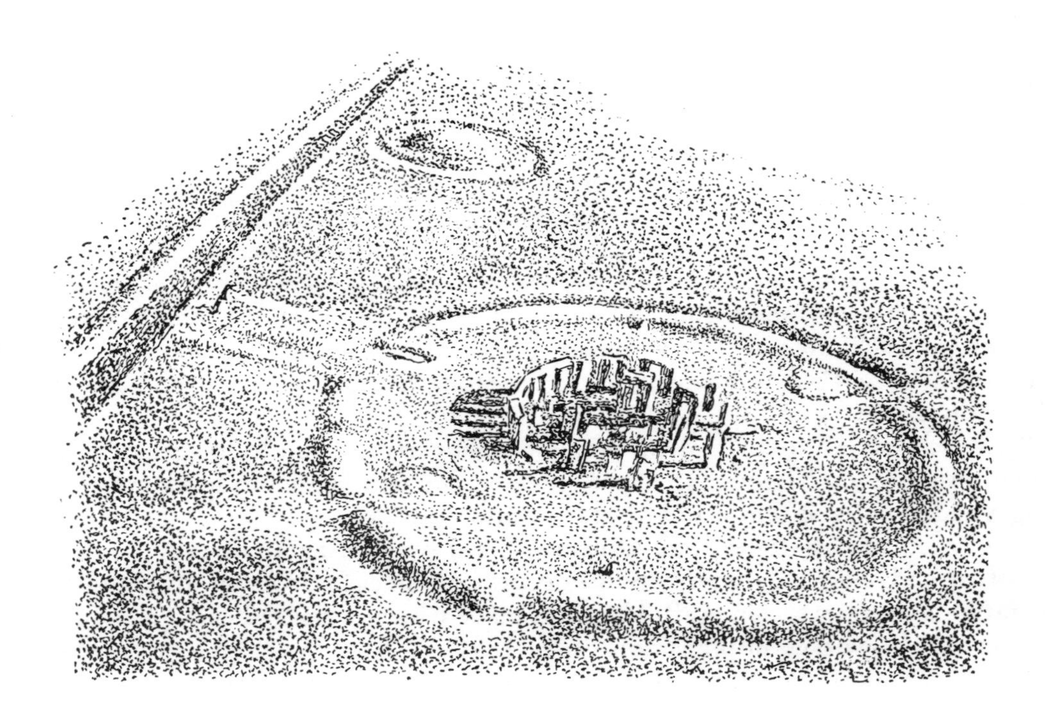

An aerial view of Stonehenge as it is today. Notice the large bank and ditch which surround the building. In the background is a round burial mound.

Building Stonehenge, Wiltshire, in the Bronze Age.

The Coming of Metals

ROUND BARROWS

The Beaker invaders brought with them a different idea of burial from that of the early farmers. Instead of making houses of the dead under long burial mounds, they buried their dead under circular earthen mounds.

The early farmers were seldom buried with any of their worldly goods, but the Beaker folk liked to have with them such things as they felt would be of use to them in the next world. In time this method of burial became the general practice; this is fortunate from our point of view since, by the things buried with them, we can judge how these people lived.

Through contact with their friends in Europe, and perhaps through traders from the Mediterranean, the people in the west of Britain had learned how to find and use a third metal – tin. By itself this was of no great importance but when tin was added in small quantities to molten copper (about one part in ten), the mixture was found to be far harder than copper by itself and much better for making tools and weapons. The Bronze Age had begun in Britain.

Bronze daggers made by local craftsmen were often put into the mound burials as well as ornaments of gold. Some of the things made of gold, however, are so well designed and executed that it is hard to believe that they were made by local smiths; it seems more likely that they were obtained through trade with people from across the Channel and originally from the Mediterranean.

One kind of ornament found in these graves was almost certainly made in Egypt or on the eastern coast of the Mediterranean. Small beads made of a substance which looks like blue china and called faience must have come from these regions. The beads are about one inch long, cylindrical and with surfaces scored at regular intervals with deep grooves. Perhaps it was with beads like this that early merchants from afar paid for the copper and tin they came to buy.

Another kind of bead quite commonly found in the round barrows was made of amber. More rarely quite large objects made of amber were buried with the dead; in one case there was a handled cup. Now, this material is found only in the northern countries of Europe. The people of Britain, then, were quite clearly carrying on trade with neighbours in northern Europe as well as with those from the more distant south-east.

In the background of this picture are a number of round barrows. They surround an earlier barrow of the long-mound type. In the foreground a group of mourners are burying a chieftain. He lies in a shallow wooden coffin and at his head is a wooden shield. Two of the men are putting into the grave a dagger and a mace. Eventually the grave will be covered with a circular earthen mound.

Bush Barrow, Stonehenge, Wiltshire. A Bronze Age burial in a round barrow.

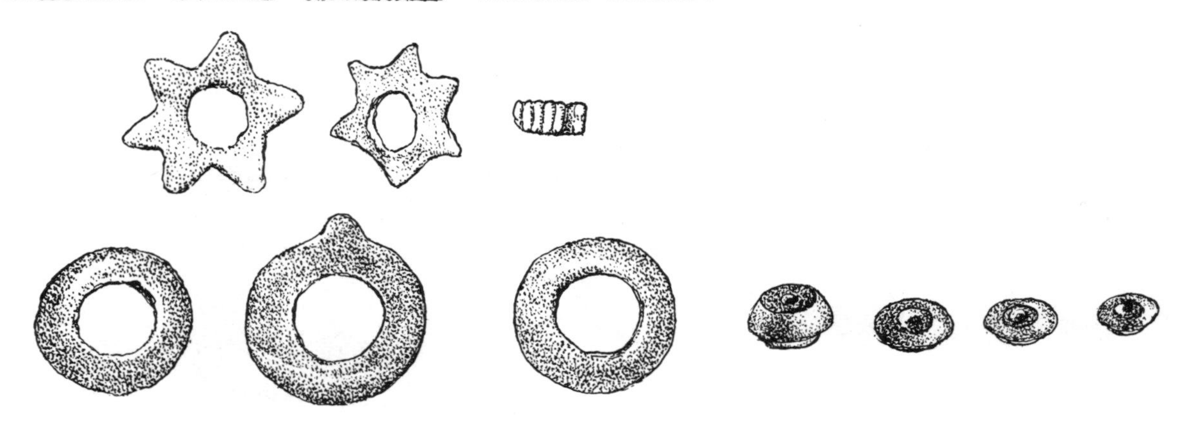

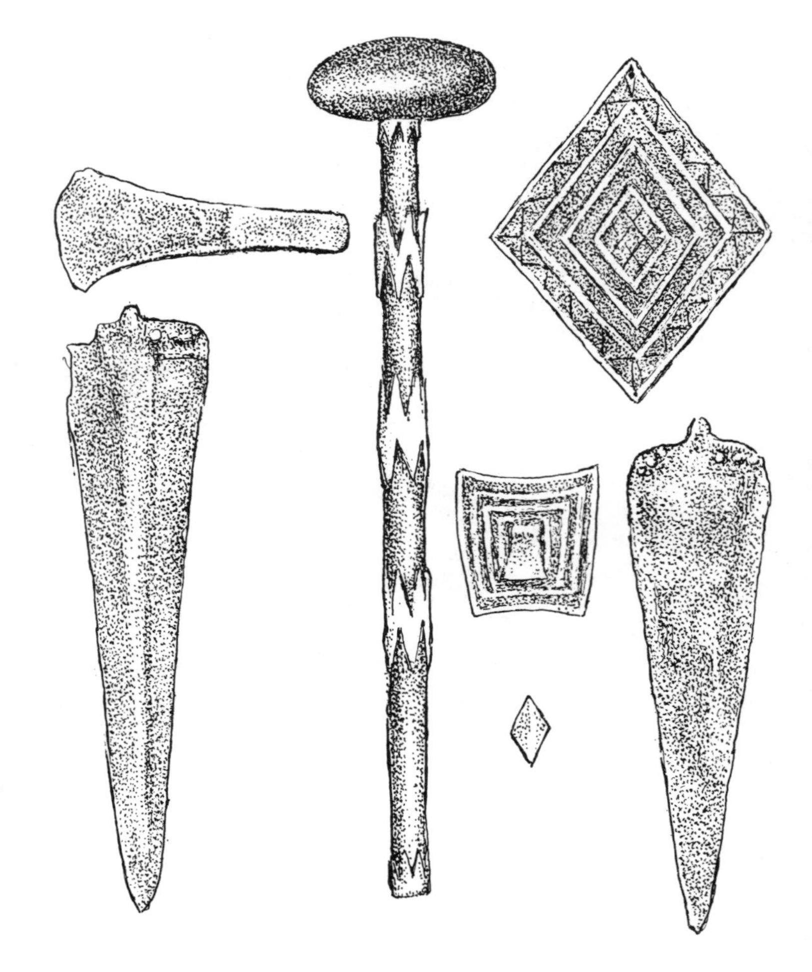

Above Beads of various shapes made of blue faience. Some were found in Syria and Egypt, others came from burials in Britain. Notice the similarity. To the right, amber beads from a burial in Somerset. The amber was probably traded from Denmark. *Right* Dagger blades and an axe-head of bronze; a stone mace with a handle ornamented with bone; and three gold ornaments. From Bush Barrow, Wiltshire.

The Bronze Age

A VILLAGE

In the thousand years that followed the arrival of the first metal-workers, the people of Britain slowly absorbed more new ideas from the Continent. Villages do not seem to have existed at first, for even the huts in which the first farmers lived were widely scattered. Dating from the Bronze Age, we find traces of small groups of houses clustered together. Unlike the earlier huts, these are circular in plan and built by setting upright posts into the ground linked together with woven sticks. The buildings were probably covered with thatched roofs.

In most places none of the wood has survived but we can still trace the places where the posts stood, since in order to make the posts stand firmly the builders had to dig deep holes into the ground. Slowly, as the wood rotted, soil slipped into these holes and when the building collapsed the holes became completely filled with top-soil. Thus when archaeologists excavate where the huts once stood they find a deep soil-filled pocket wherever a post was set up; the plan of the house can thus be known.

In these villages, each house or group of houses was fenced off to enclose a small area that may have been either a garden or a farmyard in which young animals could be kept close to the dwellings. Some of the buildings must have been storehouses, workshops and cattle-sheds, indeed, in many cases less than half of the huts were dwelling houses. The population of a village can therefore have only been quite small, possibly with no more than would be provided by the members of a large family.

Beyond the village lay the cultivated fields, the old boundaries (as banks and ditches) of which can often still be seen. Although no ploughs of any kind have been found we know that these people owned them, for occasionally, underneath the soil on which their burial barrows were built, we find traces of furrows which could only have been made by hand-drawn ploughs.

During the Bronze Age barley was a very important crop. As a way of preserving the grain from spoiling during storage it was put into deep pits dug into the ground; these pits were lined with basket-work and covered over with straw and a thin layer of earth. When such storage pits are found by archaeologists it is not uncommon for them to find some grain still remaining.

Sometimes the pits became no longer usable because moulds grew in them; when this happened the people very often just used them as rubbish tips and in such pits are often found broken tools and pottery, as well as meat bones. From these remains we learn much of how the people lived.

Nestling in a combe on the South Downs, and surrounded by fields of barley, we see in our picture a village of small thatched huts. They are surrounded by palisades. A shepherd boy with his dog keeps an eye on the small, horned sheep.

The reconstructed form of one of the huts from Itford Hill, Sussex. All that the archaeologists had to work from in making this reconstruction were ten post-holes in the ground, but the structure is based upon primitive huts made by people in parts of the world today. *Right* Actual ears of Bronze Age barley from a storage pit at Itford Hill. They are so well preserved because they had become partly charred.

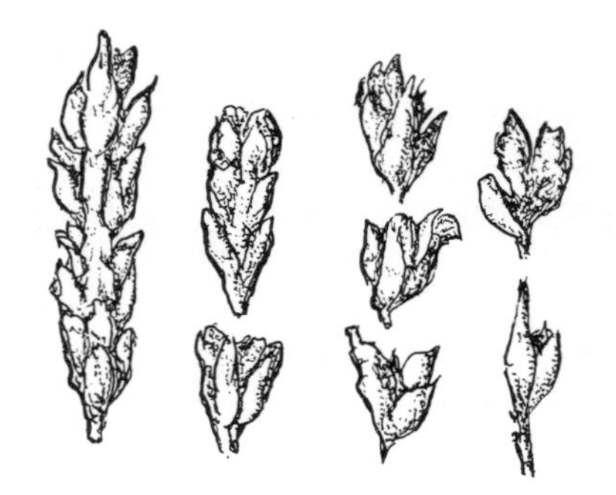

Itford Hill Sussex. A Bronze Age village with sheep.

The Bronze Age

THE BRONZE-SMITHS

Gradually during this period the use of bronze became more common. It was used to make a variety of tools and weapons and there were two sources of supply. Copper and tin came in from the hilly areas of Ireland, Scotland and the west of Britain in increasing quantities; and old, worn-out and broken tools were collected, melted down and made into new implements.

The collection of scrap-metal seems to have been a highly organised business. Because it was heavy stuff to carry the travelling merchants had secret hiding places where they hid their scrap bronze until the time came for melting it down and making new tools. A large number of these dumps have been found, and from the bits and pieces in them we are able to know how the early bronze-smiths worked.

The scrap was broken down into small pieces, no doubt by hitting it with a heavy stone, and the fragments were put into a deep clay cup. This had then to be heated until the bronze became molten, so the cup was placed in the middle of a charcoal fire which was blown to a bright red heat by bellows.

The bronze-smith would have already prepared a tool-shaped mould into which the molten metal was to be poured. The mould would be of clay or stone, or even of bronze. It was heated and set upright by partly burying it in the ground. Then the smith would take a freshly-cut stick, bend it so that he could grasp the cup containing the liquid metal and, quickly while it was still hot, he would pour the bronze into the mould.

On cooling the metal became solid and when the mould was cold it was opened and the new bronze tool was removed. It would be polished with a block of sandstone. If it was to have a cutting edge, like a knife or an axe-head, this would be made by hammering.

A few objects were made entirely by hammering thin pieces of metal into even thinner sheets, which were bent, trimmed and hammered further into shape. All this work must have been carried out on a wooden anvil. For shaping, stones were used as hammers; punches and other shaping tools were made of hard wood or bone.

The boy kneeling by the fire in the picture is working a pair of skin bellows to bring the fire to a good red heat. His companion is pouring molten bronze into a mould buried in the ground. Behind them, two craftsmen are decorating a bronze shield by hammering it on a wooden anvil and using a bone punch.

The bronze-smith at work (typical of Yorkshire and Sussex).

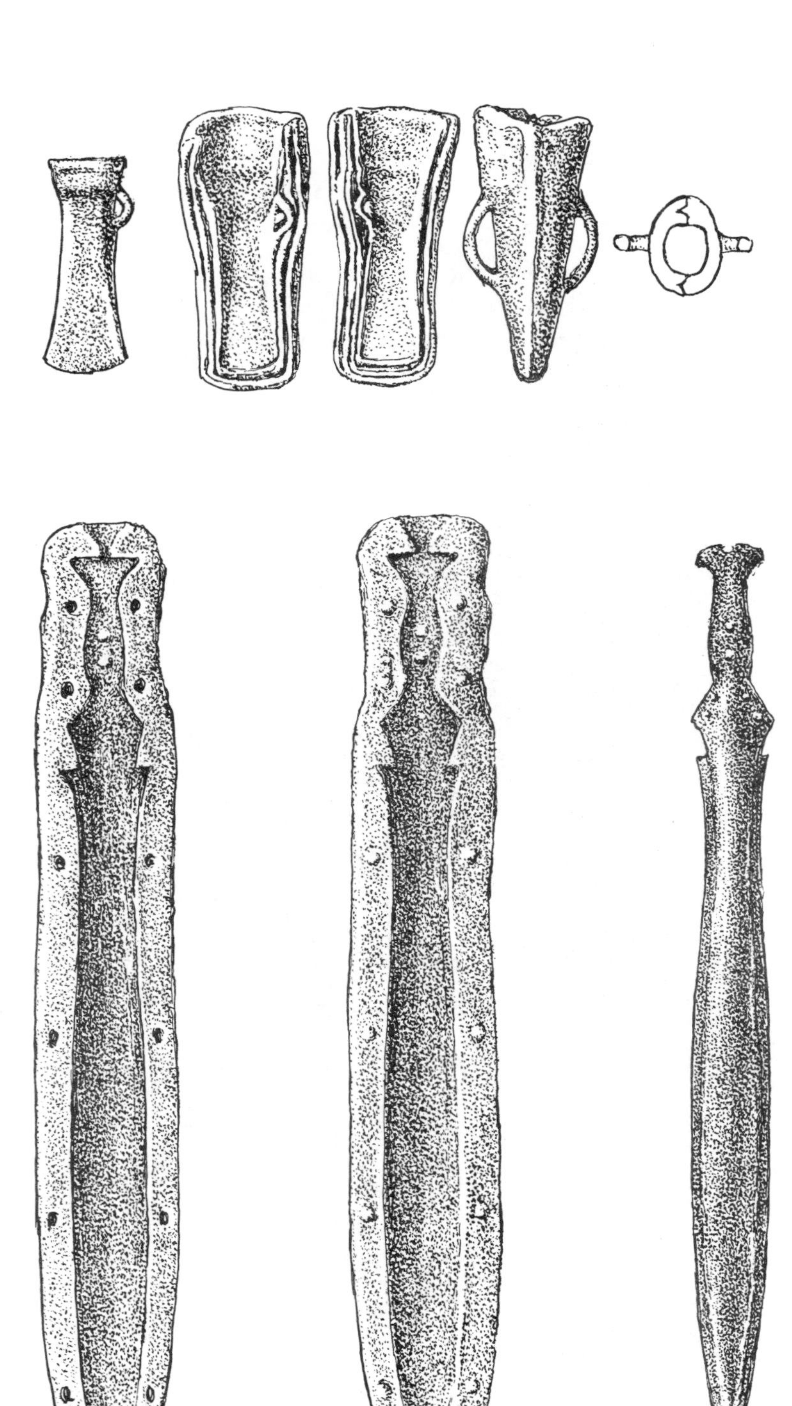

Above A mould made of bronze from Wilmington, Sussex. On the right is a view of the two segments as put together for casting. It would have been lashed together through the loops. On the left is an axe-head such as might have been made in the mould. *Below* A reconstruction of a mould made of clay and used for casting swords. The fragments from which this reconstruction was made were found at Fimber in Yorkshire. Notice the funnel at the top of the mould into which the molten metal was poured, and the way in which the two parts were made to fit accurately together by means of knobs and sockets. On the right is a sword from the River Thames at Brentford made in such a mould.

Above left A bronze shield from Coveney Fen, Cambridgeshire. *Right* A bronze sword from the River Thames at Richmond. Originally it would have had a wooden or bone grip, but this has decayed. *Centre* A bronze spear-head from Maentwrog, Merionethshire. This would have been mounted on a wooden shaft, probably of ash wood. *Below* A large bronze cauldron from County Tyrone, Ireland. When full to the brim it would have held about eight gallons.

The Bronze Age

WARRIORS AND WEAPONS

During the Bronze Age a great number of tools were developed in Britain, or the designs were brought over from other European countries. The most common was an axe-head made with a hollow socket so that it could fit over the short arm of a forked stick – the other, longer arm serving as a handle. These axe-heads were made with a small loop of metal at the side so that they could be tied firmly to the handle. Even if we knew nothing else about these people we could guess from the great number of axe-heads alone that they spent much of their time cutting down timber and in wood-carving. We know that they made canoes in much the same way as the early farmers, but by using bronze axes they certainly made the work of hollowing out a tree-trunk simpler and quicker.

Other bronze tools that have been discovered include chisels, gouges, sickles, knives and even small razors. A great number of bronze weapons was also made. Spearheads, which were very common, may have been used in hunting wild animals, but swords which were also made in great numbers,clearly suggest warfare. Indeed, although the small villages that have been discovered show that many people were living quiet and peaceful lives, the bronze weapons can only mean that there was also a great deal of unrest. Probably local chieftains were in the habit of going out on raiding expeditions to steal their neighbours' goods and animals.

On such a war-party the wealthier warriors would carry bronze shields, while other swordsmen would carry shields made of ox-hide. The bronze shields that have been found are made of rather thin metal and were probably of not much use against spears and swords, but they would deflect arrows and stones thrown from a sling.

It was probably the same wealthy warrior chieftains who owned the large bronze cauldrons that have been found. Made of many sheets of hammered bronze rivetted together, they sometimes measure more than two feet across and were able to hold an enormous stew. We can imagine how, after a successful raid, the chief would regale his followers with a great feast served from his cauldron.

We see in our picture, landing from a dug-out canoe, a raiding party armed with swords and spears of bronze. The shields being carried by the three men in the lead are also of bronze. It was still often quicker to travel by river than by land.

A raiding party in the Fens.

The Bronze Age
WEAVING AND CLOTHING

We have very little idea of how people made their clothes or dressed in the periods before the Bronze Age in Britain, but from then on we begin to find heavy clay weights with holes through them on the floors of the houses. Very occasionally these weights have been discovered lying in neat rows, and this allows us to say that they were part of a loom on which cloth was woven. Naturally all the wooden parts of the loom have vanished, so, too, has the thread, but we can see from a picture on a Greek decorated cup how such a loom worked.

One set of threads, hung from a cross-bar high on a wooden frame, was kept tightly drawn by weights attached at the lower ends. Into this set of threads was woven another thread which was wrapped round a bobbin passed to and fro from side to side. From time to time this horizontal thread would have to be pushed up hard to make the cloth firm and, for this purpose, a small bone comb was used. Because bone survives better in some soils than wood, a number of combs have lasted until this day and we can be fairly sure that they were used in weaving, since they are nearly always found close to loom weights.

We would know very little about clothes from cloth made at this time if we had to rely entirely on the few small fragments that have been found in Britain, but a number of discoveries have been made in Denmark that allow us to be pretty sure of the kind of clothes people wore during this period. Garments in exceptionally good condition have been found in burials discovered in the Danish peat-bogs.

The men wore tunics that fell to just above their knees and were gathered at the waist by a belt. Over this they wore a cloak fastened at the shoulder by a large bronze pin; on their heads they wore round, brimless hats. On their feet they had very simple leather shoes.

Women wore a short shirt reaching down to the waist, with sleeves covering the upper arms. They also had short skirts hanging to just above the knee. These skirts were not of woven cloth; they were skilfully made as a fringe of heavy tassels.

The clothes of both men and women were woven from sheep's wool, but in some cases hair from deer was mixed with it. A small fragment of cloth from Ireland was made of horse hair. Clearly garments of this period must have been rather rough to wear, but they also had to be tough.

The picture shows a wooden loom set up inside a hut. The threads running from the bar at the top are held taut by clay weights while the weaver passed her bobbin to and fro. Notice the short-sleeved shirts and the tasselled skirts worn by the women.

Weaving on a frame loom.

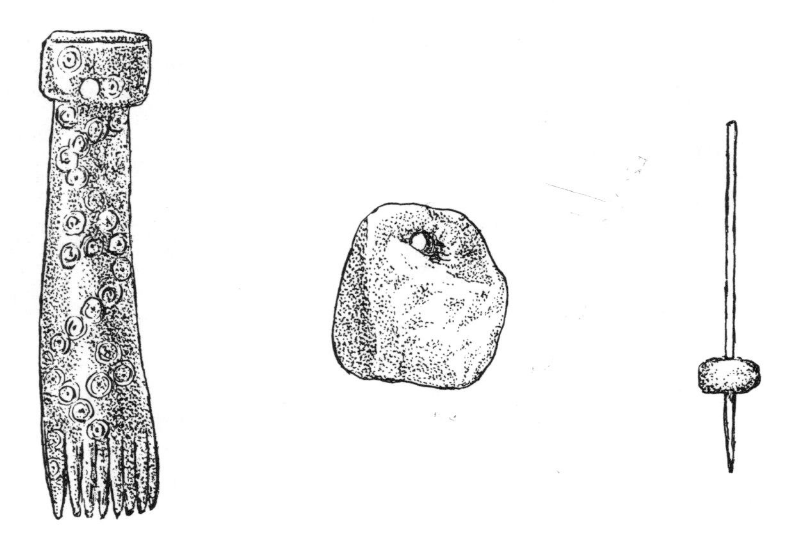

Above A weaving comb from Danebury, Hampshire; it was made of bone and was used to pack the threads tightly during weaving. A chalk loom-weight and a spindle used for making thread, from Maiden Castle, Dorset. *Below* A painting made on a cup by a Greek painter of this period. Behind the standing woman can be seen a loom of the kind shown in the large picture.

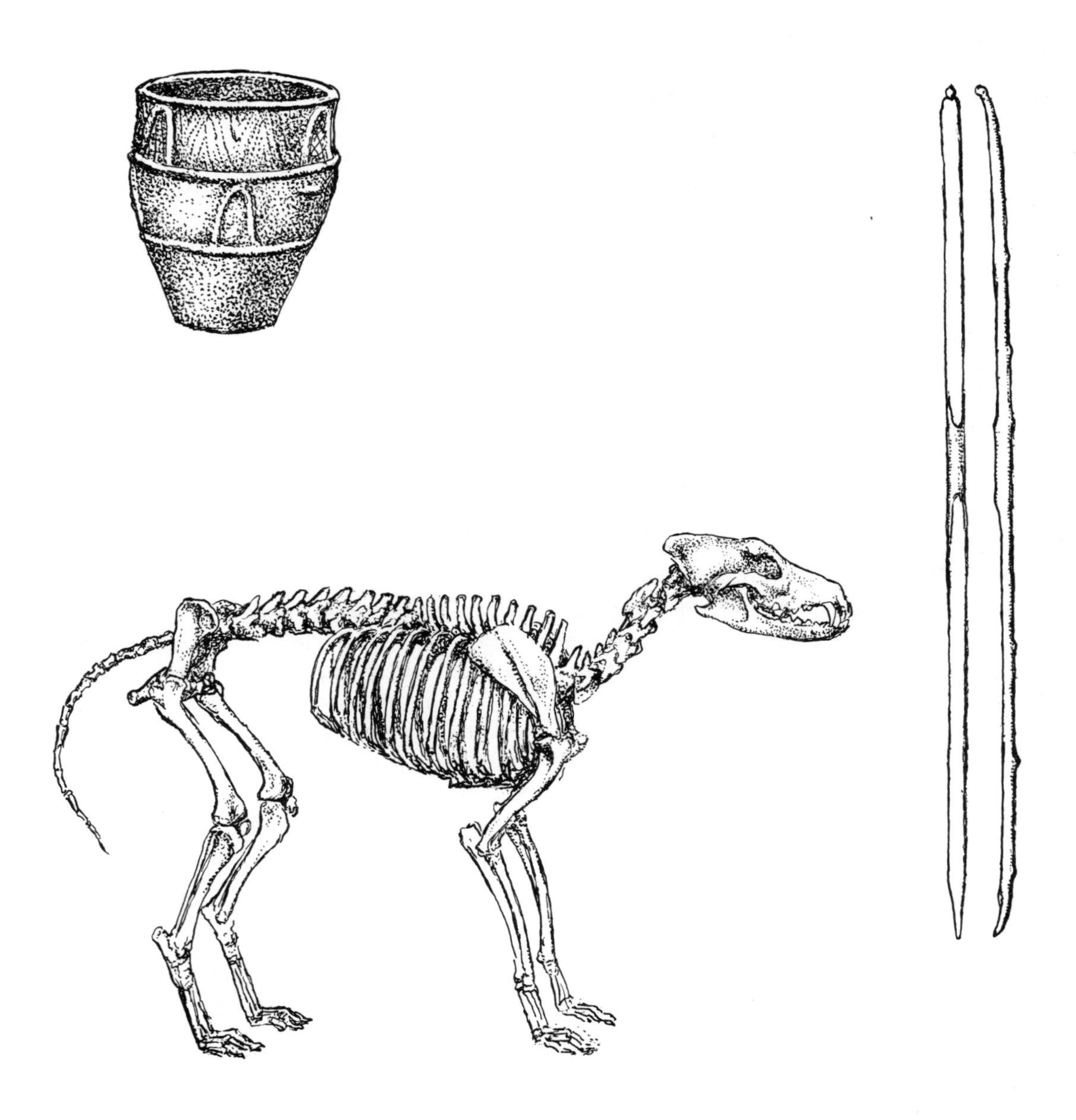

Above One of the many kinds of burial urn used after cremation during the Bronze Age. This one comes from Nether Swell in Gloucestershire. *Below* The skeleton of a dog of the kind buried with the hunter at Snail Down, Wilts. This skeleton, however, came from Windmill Hill in Wiltshire. *Right* A wooden bow from Edgington Burtle, Somerset. It is unusually well preserved. Such a bow was buried with the ashes of the hunter at Snail Down.

The Bronze Age

THE BURNING AND BURIAL

We saw how, with the coming of metals, new ideas about burying the dead came into fashion. Slowly yet another idea gained popularity during the early part of the Bronze Age. The body was placed upon a large pyre of wood which was then set on fire. The fire was fierce enough to burn away everything except the bones which, even so, became very brittle. When the fire had died down the cremated bones were removed and crushed into small pieces.

Meanwhile a suitable pottery vessel had been made ready and into it were placed the crushed bones. The pottery urns used for this purpose were very like the jars used in the villages for storing food-stuffs but were often more elaborately decorated.

The urns containing the burnt bones were then buried. The manner of burying them varied. Sometimes the urn was placed in a pit and a low mound of soil thrown up over it; sometimes the urn was just placed on the surface and covered with a mound; sometimes the urn was buried in the ground without any mound over it at all; and quite often the urn was put into a hole dug into an existing burial barrow.

Curiously, the urn was not always put into the ground the right way up. In fact it is very common to find these urns upside down and covering the small pile of burnt bones.

The habit of burying useful objects with the dead went on for a time. Thus in one burial the heads of the arrows which belonged to the dead man, as well as the skeleton of his dog, were found; so we must suppose that he had been a great hunter and that his weapons and his favourite hound were buried with him for use in the after-life.

In the picture the pyre has begun to burn down and when it is cool enough the ashes of the dead huntsman will be placed in an urn and buried in the pit seen in the foreground. With them will be laid his bow and arrows and the body of his hound. This burial was excavated by archaeologists at Snail Down in Wiltshire.

Snail Down, Wiltshire. A hunter's cremation and burial in a round barrow, with a dog, deer's antlers and bow and arrows.

The Iron Age

FARMING

While the people of Britain and other countries in Western Europe were still using bronze tools the discovery had been made, again in the Near East, of how to use an even more useful metal – iron. The knowledge of how to make iron tools and weapons spread across Europe and eventually small bands of people who had this knowledge began to settle in different parts of Britain, bringing with them many fresh ideas.

Although still circular in plan, the houses of these new settlers were considerably more solid than those of the people of the Bronze Age; their iron axes made tree-felling and wood-working easier and they could therefore afford to be more ambitious in their buildings. Often we find that they lived in single, isolated farmhouses rather than in villages, each group of farm buildings being surrounded by a heavy wooden stockade made of posts set in the ground.

Methods of farming seem to have changed little, although we do know that a more substantial plough was used; what is more, we can be fairly confident of its appearance. Once again, we must turn to the remarkably well preserved wooden objects from the peat-bogs of Denmark, in which actual ploughs have been found. The plough was pulled by a pair of oxen.

The wood for the plough-beam was carefully selected so that, although it was straight for most of its length, it curved downwards at the rear. In the end of the beam was a deep slot and into this fitted a sharp, sometimes iron-tipped, point – the share – which, drawn through the soil, made a furrow for the planting of grain. The share was held into its slot in the beam by a wedge; the handle by the which the ploughman controlled the plough was fitted and wedged into the same slot.

These ploughs were quite different from those in use today, which turn the soil over as they move forward; Iron Age ploughs made a furrow only by pushing the soil apart, and although this kind of plough may seem crude it took much of the hard work out of farming.

The picture shows part of the stockaded farmstead at Little Woodbury in Wiltshire. Through the gateway can be seen the farmer ploughing and his wife sits on the ground outside their house grinding corn. With her left hand she pours grain into the mill and with the other she turns the upper stone; a mat catches the flour as it falls from the mill.

Little Woodbury, Wiltshire. Grinding corn in a quern.

For the housewife the coming of a new type of corn-mill must have been a great blessing. The upper stone no longer had to be pushed backwards and forwards; instead it was shaped in such a way that it turned on the fixed lower stone. A hole was bored into the upper stone so that a wooden handle for turning it could be fitted. The grain was poured into another hole in the middle of the upper stone; it then found its way between the two stones where it was ground. Finally it poured out at the edges of the two stones as flour.

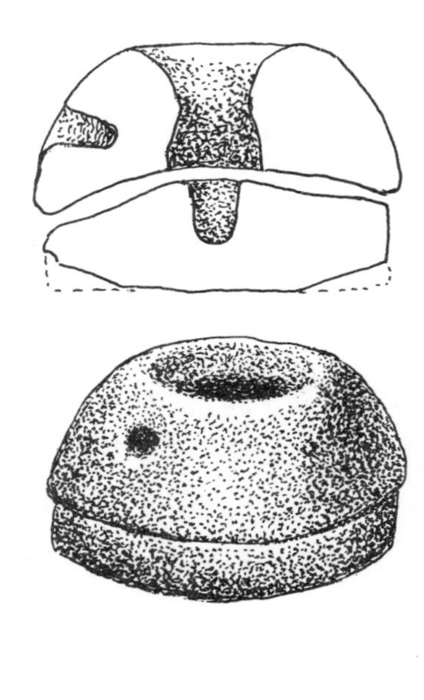

Right A stone corn-mill from Maiden Castle, Dorset. The upper picture shows the mill in section. When in use a wooden peg would have been set in the socket in the centre of the lower half to act as an axle around which the upper half could turn. The socket in the side of the upper stone was for the turning handle. *Below* A complete wooden plough from a peat bog in Denmark. The share and handle, seen on the right, are set into a slot cut in the curved draught-beam. A short wooden peg would pass through the hole at the other end of the beam to hold the lashings of the ox-yoke.

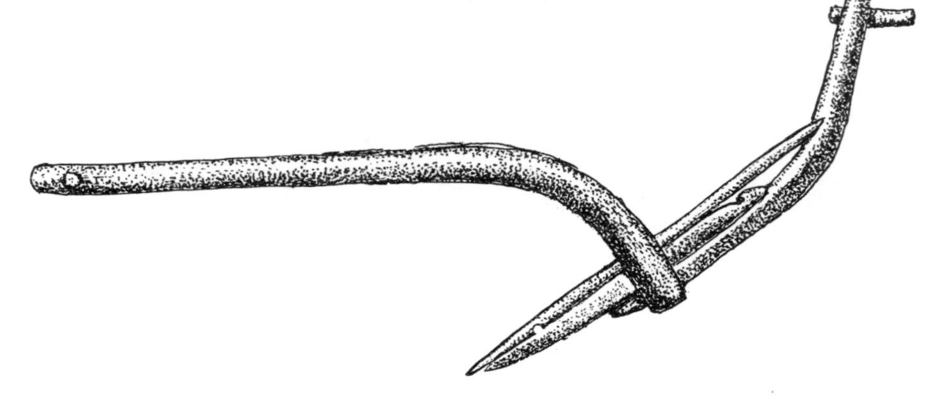

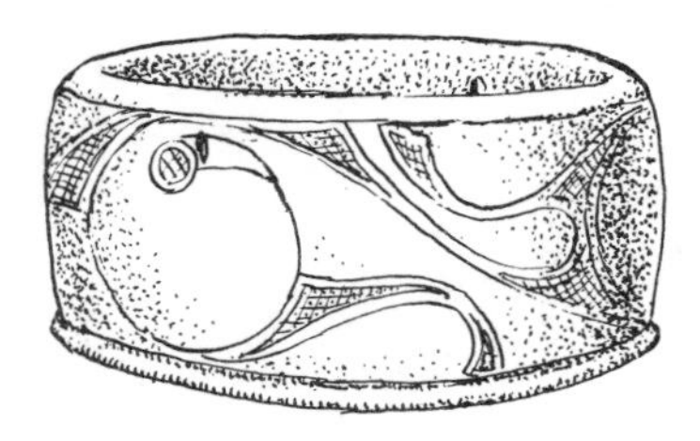

Left An Iron Age wooden bowl from Glastonbury, Somerset. It was made on a lathe and the decoration was later added by carving. *Right* Two Iron Age jars from Swarling, Kent. If they are compared with pottery vessels shown earlier in this book, it will be seen how much finer and more shapely they are.

The Iron Age

THE POTTER'S WHEEL AND THE LATHE

The rotary mill was not the only invention which made use of the rotating wheel, brought to Britain during the Iron Age; both the potter's wheel and the wood-turner's lathe came in during this period. The potter's wheel and the lathe were both made largely of wood and no remains survive, but the pottery and the turned wooden bowls which were produced on them have been preserved; they are so even and regular in shape that they can only have been made in this way. Once again we have to rely on Greek and Egyptian pictures of this period to help us to know what these things were like.

The potter's wheel would have had a large horizontal fly-wheel near the ground; this wheel was connected by a shaft to a smaller, upper wheel on which the potter placed his clay. The two wheels and the shaft were held in a simple wooden frame on which the potter could also sit. By kicking the lower-wheel, the potter could make his lump of clay spin rapidly and he could then shape vessels quickly. Not only could pots be made more quickly but they were thinner and more evenly finished; and the potter could use finer clay and so produce more attractive bowls and jars.

The lathe was used for making wooden bowls and dishes as well as handles for tools. The wood to be shaped was fixed between two horizontal spindles held in a wooden frame. A cord was tied to a springy tree-branch above, passed round one of the spindles and was tied at the lower end to a treadle. When the wood-worker pressed down with his foot on the treadle the cord would be pulled tight; at the same time, the cord, wrapped as it was round the spindle, would make it turn and the piece of wood being shaped would turn also.

Then when the wood-worker took his foot off the treadle the cord would be free to move up as the tree-branch flew up again. Then the wood-worker would press his foot down again and each time he did so the wood would turn; and, as it did, the man working the lathe would shave the block of wood nearer to the shape he wanted. Only rounded objects could be made in this way, but, when finished, they were always more regular than those made by hand. The few wooden objects that we have from this period have an elegance impossible to achieve before the coming of the lathe.

The picture shows a potter at his wheel in the shade of a tree in the foreground. As he kicks the fly-wheel with his right foot he shapes a jar on the smaller wheel to which it is connected. Beyond him can be seen a wood-worker shaving down a block of wood on the lathe to produce a bowl.

Wheel-made pottery and Iron Age wood turning.

The Iron Age
IRON FORGING

The use of iron instead of bronze for the making of tools and weapons called for a series of completely new techniques. Bronze could be heated until it melted and then be poured into prepared shaping moulds, but this could not be done with iron for it was impossible at this time to produce a fire hot enough to melt the new metal. Instead the iron had to be made red-hot in a forge and then, while still hot, it had to be shaped on an anvil. The red-hot iron had to be held in tongs and struck with a heavy iron hammer.

Iron had many advantages over bronze. In the first place it was simpler to join one piece of iron to another than to join bronze. If two pieces of red-hot iron are placed together on an anvil and struck hard they will weld. This fact allowed the making of quite complicated objects, many of which have been discovered; and some of them look surprisingly 'modern'.

In addition, iron can be obtained much more easily than copper and tin, for the rocks from which it can be extracted are far more widely found. This meant, of course, that it was possible for people who could not afford tools made of bronze to buy – or even make – tools of iron. Metal tools and weapons became far more common.

A second and more far-reaching effect of the use of iron was that it allowed people to design tools for particular purposes rather than having to make do with a few, simple all-purpose ones. For example we find special knives being made for leather workers, shears for cutting wool and a wide variety of axes and swords.

For many purposes, however, iron was not suitable and it could not be so finely and decoratively worked as bronze. As a result bronze continued to be used for the making of many things – buttons, brooches, buckles, shields, helmets and the metal fittings for horse harness, all of which would have been very difficult to make in iron.

In the picture the older of the boys is holding red-hot fire-dogs with a pair of tongs on top of a stone anvil while the blacksmith forges them into shape with an iron-headed hammer. The younger boy works a pair of bellows so that the fire will be hot enough to re-heat the metal.

Forging an iron fire-dog.

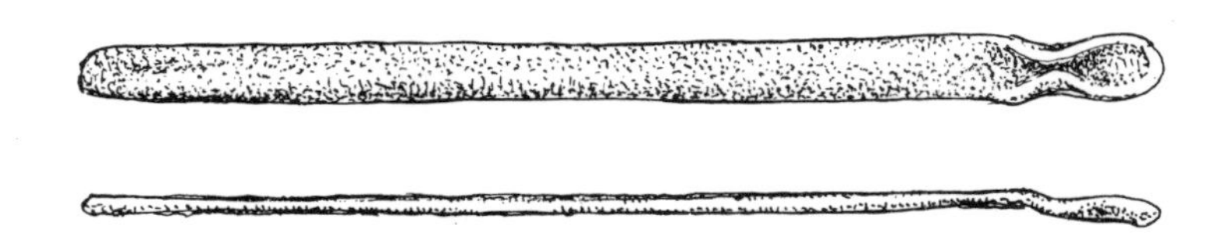

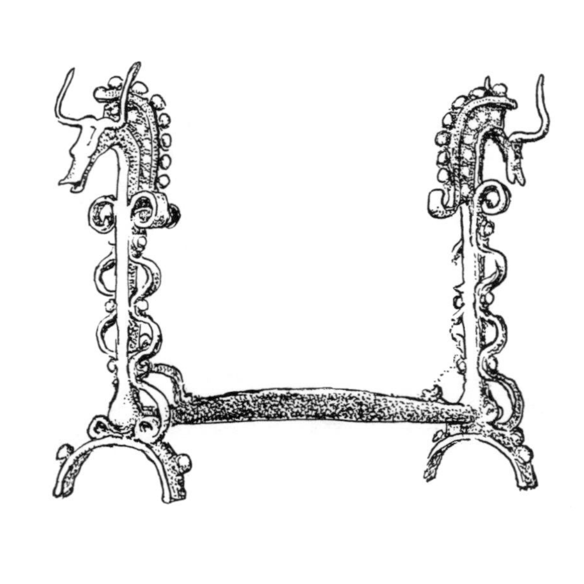

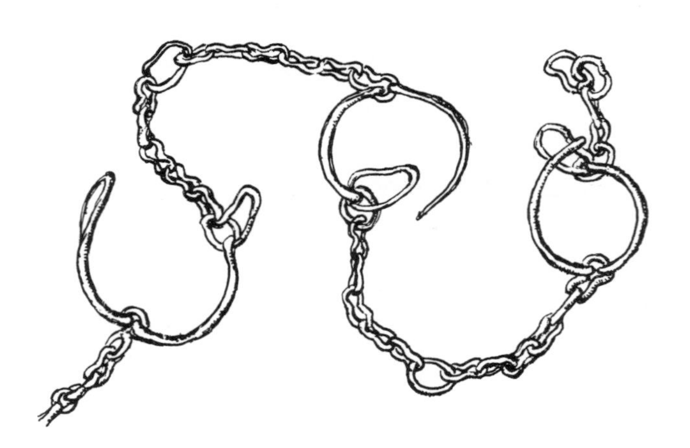

Top An iron bar found at Bourton-on-the-Water, Gloucestershire. This was the shape in which iron was traded across the country: an iron bar with a 'neck' to which string could be tied to make it simpler to carry. Later it would be forged into tools, weapons and other objects. *Centre* An iron fire-dog from Capel, Denbighshire. A good example of the elaborate iron-work of this age. A pair of such dogs would be used to support the logs on the hearth. *Bottom* An iron chain from Barton in Cambridgeshire; it was used to manacle slaves or prisoners.

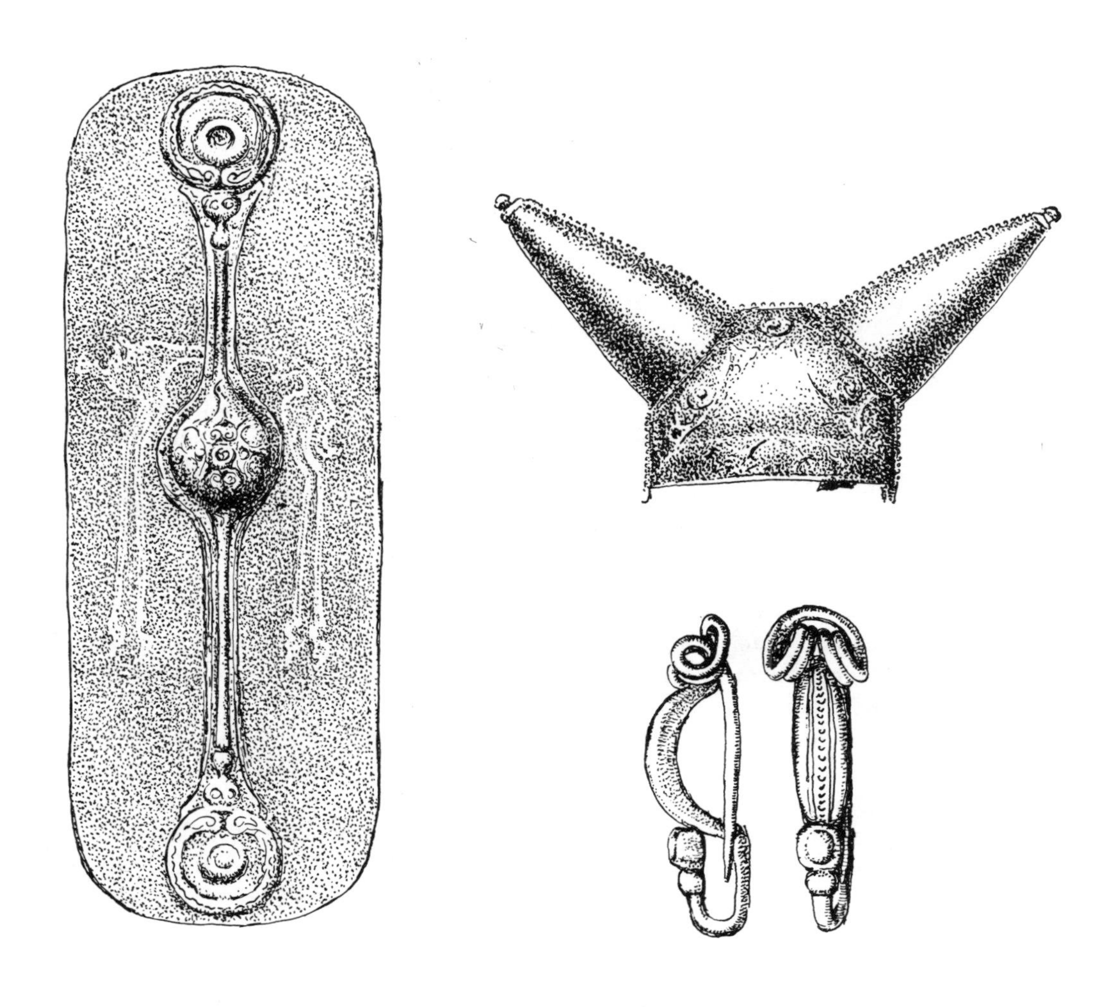

Above left A bronze shield from Witham, Essex. Apart from the three bronze 'bosses' it was decorated with a picture of a wild boar, probably of applied sheet metal rivetted to the surface. This was removed before the bosses were added, leaving a 'print' on the surface of the shield. *Above right* A bronze helmet from the River Thames. It was made of four pieces of hammered sheet metal joined with rivets. *Centre* Two views of a bronze cloak-pin, from Blandford, Dorset. It worked exactly as a modern safety-pin; the pin point was pushed through the cloth and held fast in the catch by the force of a coil spring.

The Iron Age
AT WAR

Horses may have been known in Britain before the coming of the people of the Iron Age but, if so, they were not used for pulling carts. During this period, however, the chariot was introduced to Britain. This was really just a two-wheeled light cart pulled by a pair of small horses and it was drawn by a single shaft lying between them. The end of the shaft was attached to a yoke that lay over the horses' shoulders and was kept in place by girths and straps round the horses' necks.

Although chariots were often used simply for getting about, their chief use was probably in warfare. Each chariot carried a crew of two, one man to drive and the other to fight, and because they could so easily attack and then quickly withdraw during battle they were a great menace to foot-soldiers.

In order to be able to meet attacks from charioteers the chieftains of the various tribes made forts in which they could take refuge. These forts were built on the tops of hills to make the approach of chariots more difficult. They were made by digging a series of deep ditches which chariots could not cross; usually on the inside was an earth and timber rampart behind which the defenders took cover, using slings to hurl stones at the attackers. Piles of sling-stones spaced at intervals round the inside of ramparts have been discovered, showing that the defenders kept themselves prepared.

As a defence against sling-stones, arrows and javelins the Iron Age warriors carried tall bronze or wood shields and on their heads wore helmets. Sometimes the helmets had a pair of horns attached and sometimes they had a crest in the form of an animal. Rather oddly they wore no body armour and the Roman general, Julius Caesar, said that they went into battle naked. By this he probably meant that they left off their cloaks and any other garments that might hinder them; to the heavily armoured Romans they would certainly have seemed naked.

The banks and ditches of the Iron Age hill-forts may still be seen today in many parts of Britain, for, being on the tops of hills, many have escaped ploughing. Even now these hill-forts are most impressive, not only by reason of the height of their banks and the depth of their ditches but because of the large areas which some of them enclosed.

The picture shows the view from the ramparts of a hill-fort under attack. The charioteers are circling the fort looking for a weak spot in the defences. Some defenders are slinging stones while the others stand ready with their spears and armour to meet the attack.

The Iron Age, a fort under attack.

The Iron Age

A WARRIOR DIES

In every period from the coming of the early farmers to the beginning of the Iron Age burial customs were highly elaborate and the graves usually marked by large mounds. The people of the Iron Age do not seem to have used such complicated rites. Indeed, in many parts of Britain no Iron Age burials have been found and we have to assume that the dead were normally either buried without any belongings in simple shallow graves or cremated and the ashes scattered.

Although simple burial was probably the normal practice there were some interesting exceptions. One group of people who settled on the Chalk Wolds of Yorkshire were buried in a most complex way. These people were obviously warriors who could not believe that, in the next world, they could do without their chariots and weapons – and of course, horses to draw the chariots.

They were buried, therefore, with their swords, their shields and their chariots, while their horses were slain and buried in the same grave, with all their harness. Perhaps these warriors were rather vain men for, rather oddly, we find also in their graves hand-mirrors made of bronze.

We know that these charioteers originally came from northern France, for similar graves have been found there, and we believe they came to Britain because other tribes from the East proved too strong for them and drove them from their homeland. It was probably for the same reason that many of the iron-using people came to Britain. Almost the whole population of Europe to the north of the Mediterranean was made up at this time of warring tribes. From time to time these tribes joined forces and attacked their Roman neighbours to the south and, on one occasion, they even reached the city of Rome itself.

The Romans decided to put an end by conquest to the danger of attack from the north and, under the able leadership of Julius Caesar, the tribes of what is France today were put down fifty years before the birth of Christ. Gaul, as it was then known, became Roman territory.

In the picture can be seen a warrior being buried with his chariot. He lies under his shield with his weapons beside him. His pair of horses have been slain and lie harnessed to the chariot, in the same grave. Two boars have been slaughtered and will be buried with him as food for his journey to the next world.

A chariot burial in Yorkshire.

Above left A bronze mirror from Desborough, Northamptonshire. This view shows the decorated back of the mirror. The other surface was originally so highly polished that it was like a looking-glass. *Above right* A bronze horse-bit from Rise in Yorkshire. It was decorated with inlays of coloured glass. *Below* A short sword from Witham, Essex. The blade was made of iron but the grip and the scabbard were of bronze.

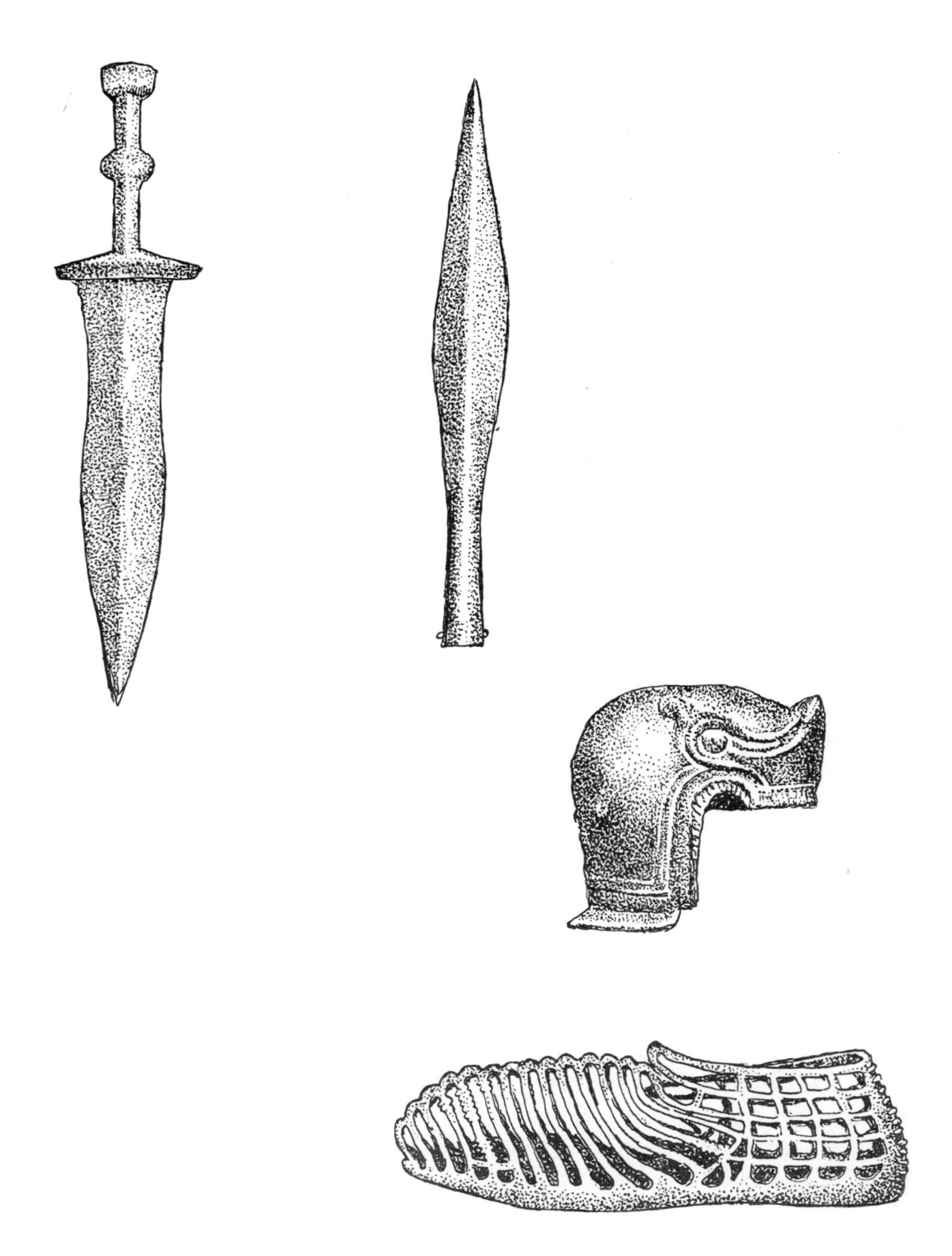

Top left A Roman short sword or dagger of iron. It was found in the hill-fort called Hod Hill in Dorset. *Top right* A Roman iron spear-head from Cloak Lane, London. It is typical of the well-made Roman weapons. *Centre* A bronze helmet from Guisborough, Yorkshire. This helmet was probably that of an officer. *Bottom* A leather sandal from London, such as might have been worn by an officer in the Roman army.

The Roman Conquest

During the conquest of Gaul by the Romans, many of the British tribes gave their support to their friends across the Channel and, once he had finished with Gaul, Caesar decided to attack Britain. Quite apart from the help they were giving the Gauls, the Britons were known by the Romans to have rich farmlands as well as a plentiful supply of copper, tin, lead and iron. So, in planning to conquer Britain, Caesar aimed both at preventing aid to the Gauls and at making his war profitable.

Caesar, however, found that he had too small an army for the task he had in mind and, although he crossed the Channel and defeated the local tribes in two years running (55 BC and 54 BC), he was never able to complete his conquest of the country. It was not until nearly one hundred years later (in AD 42) that the Emperor Claudius felt that he had enough troops available to ensure success.

The British tribes were far from united; if they had been, the Roman army might have found its task much more difficult, if not impossible. Some tribes gave in immediately, their chieftains becoming puppet rulers under the Romans. Other tribes were more stubborn, but their light weapons and chariots were no match for the heavily armoured and well-disciplined Roman troops. Within two years the whole of England south of Lincoln had been conquered and, from then on the Romans gradually gained Wales, the north of England and, for a time, the lowlands of Scotland.

The history of the conquest has been recorded, of course, by Roman historians. Occasionally the truth of their statements can be checked by archaeologists. For instance we are told that tribes of south western England put up an obstinate fight, the Roman general having to fight thirty battles and to capture more than twenty hill-forts. One such fortified hill was the stupendous Maiden Castle in Dorset, whose great series of deep ditches and high earthen banks were a serious obstacle to the Romans.

Protected by volley after volley of iron-headed darts from machine catapults the Roman soldiers stormed the fort and slaughtered men, women and children. The hastily-dug graves of the wretched defenders, whose skeletons still bear the ghastly wounds of war, have been found by archaeologists and tell us the end of this grim tale.

So Britain became a Roman Province – and History had begun.

The picture shows the last stages of a Roman assault on an Iron Age hill-fort. The defenders have already been under attack from the Roman catapults and many have been killed or severely wounded. The heavily-armoured Romans are preparing to storm the gateway.

The coming of the Romans.

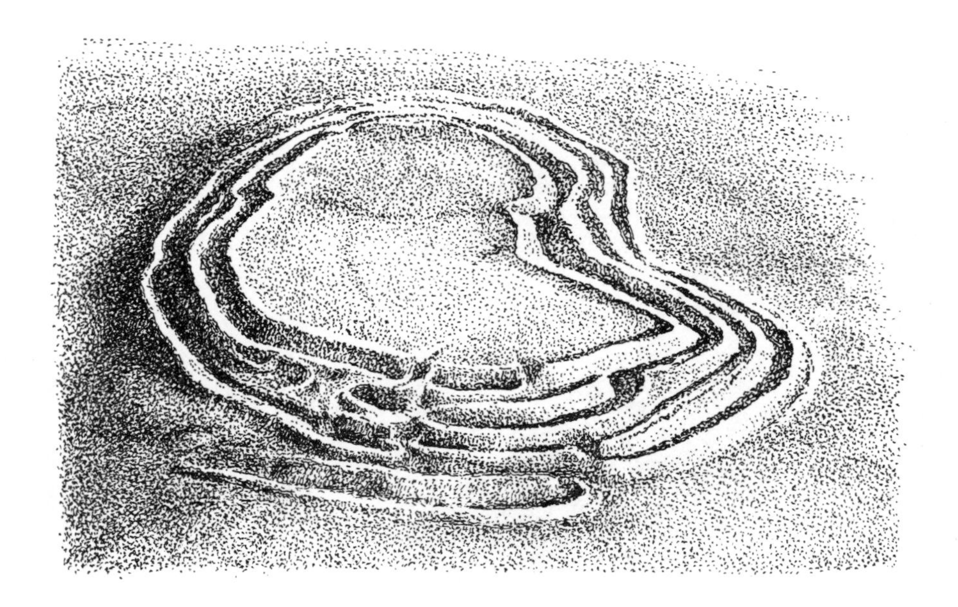

Above A view of Maiden Castle, Dorset, seen from the air as it is today. The hill-fort measures more than three-quarters of a mile from one end to the other. *Below* Part of the backbone of one of the skeletons of the defenders of Maiden Castle. The iron head of a bolt shot from a catapult can be seen lodged in the spine.